COUPERIN

L'ART DE TOUCHER LE CLAVECIN
(The Art of Playing the Harpsichord)

EDITED AND TRANSLATED BY MARGERY HALFORD

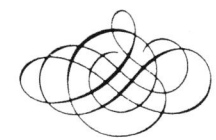

Facsimiles from Couperin's
original edition of 1716
plus a new English translation
printed parallel with
the complete texts of the
original editions of 1716 and 1717.
The music is newly engraved in
dark print with editorial suggestions
added in *lighter print*.

AN ALFRED MASTERWORK EDITION

Second Edition
Copyright © MMVIII by Alfred Publishing Co., Inc.
All rights reserved. Printed in USA.

Cover art: Interior with a Lady at a Harpsichord, *1895*
by Francesco Fieravino (Maltese, b.1640)
Oil on Canvas
Rafael Valls Gallery / The Bridgeman Art Library, London

TABLE OF CONTENTS

FOREWORD

Biographical note	3
Origin and Description of Sources	4
Facsimile of Second Prelude	6
Early Traditions in Music Writing	7
The Variable Dot	8
Inequality	8
Ornamentation	12
Fingering, Phrasing and Articulation	21
Expression and Style	23
Summary of Couperin's Rules	25
Bibliography and Acknowledgments	26

L'ART DE TOUCHER LE CLAVECIN

Title Page of the First Original Edition (1716)	27
Prefaces to the Original Editions	28
Plan of this Method	29
Reflections	32
A Little Essay on the Style of Fingering for Reaching an Understanding of the Ornaments Which Will be Found Later	33
Ornaments Used in Playing	34
Reasons for Preferring the New Fingering on Lower Appoggiaturas	38
Evolutions or Little Exercises for Training the Hands	40
Allemande	47
Sundry Advice	49
Passages in My First Book of Harpsichord Pieces Which are Difficult to Finger	51
First Prelude	56
Second Prelude	58
Third Prelude	60
Fourth Prelude	62
Fifth Prelude	64
Sixth Prelude	67
Observations	70
Seventh Prelude	71
Eighth Prelude	74
Passages from my Second Book of Pieces Which are Ambiguous in Fingering	77

APPROBATION

	84

LIST OF FACSIMILES

Second Prelude (Original Edition of 1716)	6
Seventh Prelude (Original Edition of 1716)	9
Explanation of Ornaments and Signs Premier Livre de Pièces de Clavecin (1713)	12, 13
Title Page (Original Edition of 1716)	27
Approbation (Original Edition of 1716)	84

FOREWORD

FRANÇOIS COUPERIN LE GRAND

(1668-1733)

The unbroken succession of organists surnamed Couperin who served at St. Gervais in Paris began with François le Grand's uncle Louis, and continued until 1826 when Gervais-François, a great-nephew, died. François le Grand inherited the post from his father who died in 1678. Since François was only eleven years old, the church authorities deputized the well known organist-composer La Lande to play for him until he reached 18, when he assumed the duties himself.

Couperin's music training, begun under his father's direction, is believed to have been continued by Thomelin, whom he succeeded as organist at the King's Chapel in 1693. The following year he was appointed music instructor to the royal children. In 1696, Louis XIV ennobled him, and in 1717 he was officially given the title *Ordinaire de la Musique* at the court. He was universally admired and his contemporaries called him *le Grand*, the Great Couperin, as early as 1710. Many composers dedicated works to him, including Montéclair, Siret and Dornel. J.S. Bach is known to have admired him above all French composers and his ornamentation seems to reflect Couperin's influence. The two are said to have maintained a lengthy correspondence on musical matters, which is, unfortunately, not known to exist today. Bach copied one of Couperin's pieces, *Les Bergeries*, into the notebook for Anna Magdalena.

Dr. Charles Burney, the celebrated English music critic and historian wrote the following about Couperin in his *General History of Music*. London 1789:

> "The great Couperin (b. 1668), who died in 1733, was not only an admirable organist but, in the styles of the times, an excellent composer for keyed-instruments. His instructions for fingering, in his L'Art de toucher le Clavecin (1716) are still good; though his pieces are so crouded (sic) and deformed by beats, trills, and shakes, that no plain note was left to enable the hearer of them to judge whether the tone of the instrument on which they were played was good or bad."

Couperin's "crouded" music was, in part, a reflection of life in the court of the Sun King where the proper public display of etiquette was more important than private morals. Protocol was so jealously guarded that, when an unauthorized courtier quickly handed the King's hat to him during a sudden thundershower at a garden party, the courtier to whom this privilege belonged felt disgraced and humiliated.

Besides *L'Art de toucher le Clavecin* and the four books of *Pièces de Clavecin* published in 1713, 1717, 1722 and 1730, Couperin's published works include organ masses, secular and sacred vocal and instrumental music, much of it composed for the court.

In the Preface of his last book of *Pièces*, he expressed the hope that his family would publish the remainder of his works, but posterity suffered a loss by their failure to do so. Couperin died in Paris on September 12, 1733, more honored during his lifetime than many composers even after death.

ORIGIN

Couperin wrote *L'Art de toucher le Clavecin*, The Art of Playing the Harpsichord, in response to many requests for further instruction in performing his *Pièces de Clavecin* (first book, 1713) correctly and with good taste. The first edition was published in Paris in 1716. Couperin himself characterized the book as being "very useful in general, but absolutely indispensable for playing my *Pièces* in the style most suitable to them." The following year the second book of *Pièces de Clavecin* was ready for publication. Couperin made some revisions and corrections on the original plates from which *L'Art de toucher le Clavecin* had been printed, wrote an entirely new Preface, added a supplement and reprinted it in 1717.

L'Art de toucher le Clavecin is one of the most important early 18th-century treatises extant, and important to all musicians today for the information it contains, not only on harpsichord technic, but on performance style, fingering, phrasing and ornamentation. The *Preludes*, which are seldom found in other collections of music, are small gems which should find a welcome place on many programs. For many years the only available edition of this work has been difficult to obtain and a corrected edition with open spacing has long been overdue.

Since no autographs are known to exist, the primary sources are the original editions of 1716 and 1717 published by Couperin himself. In the preparation of the present volume, all of the following sources have been consulted.

1. Couperin's first original edition, *L'Art de toucher le Clavecin* published in Paris, 1716. Microfilm courtesy of the *Bibliothèque Nationale*. Facsimiles from this edition are reproduced on pages 6, 9, 27 and 84 of the present volume.

2. The revised, corrected edition with supplement published by Couperin in 1717.

3. *L'Art de toucher le Clavecin*. A tri-lingual edition published by Breitkopf and Härtel. Portions of the *Explication des Agrémens et des Signes* from the *Premier Livre de Pièces de Clavecin* is included. Wiesbaden, 1933.

4. *The Interpretation of the Music of the XVII and XVIII Centuries*, by Arnold Dolmetsch. *The Appendix of Twenty-Two Pieces*, published separately as a companion volume. London, 1915. Many passages from *L'Art de toucher le Clavecin* and some of the illustrative fingering examples are contained in the textbook. The *First, Second* and *Fourth Preludes* are included in the Appendix.

5. *Explication des Agrémens et des Signes*. Explanation of Ornaments and Signs. Couperin refers to this Table of Ornaments and explains some of them in detail in *L'Art de toucher le Clavecin*. Facsimile from the *Premier Livre de Pièces de Clavecin*, courtesy of the Syndics of the Fitzwilliam Museum, Cambridge.

Each of these sources is further described on the following pages.

1. THE ORIGINAL EDITION OF 1716

L'Art de toucher le Clavecin is a loosely organized instruction book containing, besides directions and exercises for developing good technic on the harpsichord, a little essay on ornamentation, fingering for some difficult passages in the *Premier Livre de Pièces de Clavecin*, an *Allemande* expressly composed for the book and eight *Preludes* for loosening the fingers and trying out an unfamiliar instrument before performing. Various reflections and observations on style, taste and manner of performing and accompanying are interspersed throughout the book.

The original edition is beautifully engraved on copper plates in a large vertical format measuring about 32.5

x 25 cm. (13"x 9¾"). The book is dedicated to King Louis XIV. Facsimiles of the *Second* and *Seventh Preludes*, title page and approbation are reproduced on pages 6, 9, 27 and 84 of the present volume by kind permission of the Bibliothèque Nationale which owns the only copy of the 1716 edition known to exist. We may infer from the approbation that the book was received enthusiastically. In English, it reads as follows:

"By order of Msgr. le Chancelier, I have studied The Art of Playing the Harpsichord by M. Couperin. The very name of so celebrated an author should recommend the book, by itself, to the public. One must be obliged to a Master who has carried his art to such a high degree of perfection to wish to teach it to others, by short Lessons, which have been the fruit of his long study and continual application. Published at Paris, March 20, 1716."

2. THE ORIGINAL EDITION OF 1717

The second edition of *L'Art de toucher le Clavecin* was published in 1717. A few sentences were added and most of the errors in the first edition were corrected. A supplement was added, consisting of fingering for some difficult passages in the second book of *Pièces de Clavecin* which was published at about the same time. All references to the first book of *Pièces* were changed to refer to both the first and second books and a completely new Preface was substituted for the original one. *L'Art de toucher le Clavecin* was then reprinted from the original copper plates with a new title page.

In the Preface to the second book of *Pièces*, Couperin offered to exchange without charge all returned copies of the 1716 edition for the new one, so the original purchasers could have the supplement. The acceptance of this generous offer may account for the lack of other existing copies of the 1716 edition.

The complete French text of the 1717 edition plus the Preface from the 1716 edition (preserving the original misspellings and archaic punctuation) is reproduced in the present volume together with a completely new English translation. All of the revisions and corrections described above have been footnoted, as well as the overlooked errors. The original order of the book has not been altered, consequently the passages from the second book of *Pièces* will be found after the *Eighth Prelude*. To assist the reader in locating some of the scattered bits of related information, a summary will be found on page 25.

3. THE BREITKOPF AND HÄRTEL EDITION

This is a reprint of the 1717 edition with the French text translated into English and German. The Preface to the 1716 edition is not included. Portions of the *Explication des Agrémens et des Signes* have been included for reference but are not translated. Although the Preludes are transcribed into treble and bass clefs, the exercises and fingering examples have been left in the original moveable C-clefs. The format of the music is quite crowded and difficult to read in places as a result. Most of the time the early traditions of notating accidentals (described on page 7) are followed. However, there is no explanation given to avoid the confusion that is the necessary result of sometimes editorially adding the extra accidental required by modern notation and sometimes failing to do so. Notes with multiple flags have been altered almost without exception, apparently to make mathematical corrections in Couperin's original text. This subject is of such great importance in proper performance of early 18th-century music and the changes which have been made alter the interpretation so radically, that it is discussed in detail on page 8.

Facsimile of the *Second Prelude*
Reproduced by permission of the Bibliothèque Nationale
(Measure numbers have been added for reference purposes)

4. THE INTERPRETATION OF THE MUSIC OF THE XVII AND XVIII CENTURIES
by Arnold Dolmetsch

THE APPENDIX OF TWENTY-TWO ILLUSTRATIVE PIECES

Arnold Dolmetsch was one of the first English writers to discuss in depth the proper performance of early music. Many passages from the text of *L'Art de toucher le Clavecin* are translated in appropriate places throughout the textbook although the original French is not given. Some of the illustrative fingering examples are quoted in the chapter dealing with early fingering methods. The *First, Second* and *Fourth Preludes* are included among the pieces in the Appendix. Various inaccuracies in this edition are mentioned in the footnotes.

5. *EXPLICATION DES AGREMENS ET DES SIGNES*

5. EXPLANATION OF ORNAMENTS AND SIGNS

In keeping with the custom of the times, Couperin printed a Table of Ornaments in the first book of *Pièces de Clavecin* as a guide to correct performance. He refers to it in *L'Art de toucher le Clavecin* and discusses some of the ornaments in greater detail than the realizations in the Table show. A facsimile of the Table has been reproduced on pages 12 and 13. It is followed by a translation and discussion of Couperin's ornamentation.

EARLY TRADITIONS IN MUSIC WRITING

The beautiful facsimile of the *Second Prelude*, reproduced on the opposite page, illustrates many early traditions in music writing. Some of these need to be explained.

MOVEABLE C-CLEF. The moveable C-clef shown on the upper line of music avoids the use of many leger lines and helps to keep each hand on the same staff while it is playing. The line on which the clef is placed is middle C. It may be used on any of the four lowest lines of the staff. For the convenience of the modern performer, the moveable C-clefs have been transcribed into treble or bass throughout the present volume.

BRACKETS. Couperin used bracket-like lines for slurs. They are shown in the Table of Ornaments, page 13, #13. He used curved lines only for ties. In the present volume they have been rendered as modern curved slurs except in situations where the diagonal lines seem to make the text clearer.

DIRECTS. The marks at the ends of lines are called *directs* and indicate the pitch of the first note on the next line of music. Although they resemble an ornament symbol used by other composers, their position on the blank staff after the bar line makes their purpose clear.

ACCIDENTALS. An accidental remains in force as long as the altered note continues to be repeated without interruption of other notes or rests in the same voice, even continuing across a bar line. In the *Second Prelude*, both middle C's in measure 2 are sharp. The B in measure 7 and the first E in measure 8 are flat. In measure 10, the effect of the sharp on the first F is cancelled by the G which intervenes before the next F. Therefore, the sharp is rewritten and continues to be effective for the next note also. A courtesy accidental is sometimes used, as shown in measure 11, but more often there is none.

For the convenience of the modern reader, all accidentals which are redundant according to modern notation have been omitted. Those which are cancelled by a modern bar line have been added to the text and a few courtesy accidentals which clarify the text have been added in light print to distinguish them from the original edition.

RHYTHMIC NOTATION OF QUICK NOTES.
Quick notes which follow dotted notes are often not written with mathematical accuracy. A discussion of the performance style associated with this notational custom will be found below, *The Variable Dot in Baroque Music*. Measure 15 of the *Second Prelude* illustrates an orthography which may have been unique with Couperin. Notes with six flags (256th notes!) are a superbly graphic representation of correct performance style.

THE VARIABLE DOT IN BAROQUE MUSIC AND COUPERIN'S INCONSISTENT NOTATION

Early writers agree that the dot beside a note in baroque music had a variable time value. C.P.E. Bach says: " . . . short notes which follow dotted ones are always shorter in execution than their notated length . . . when four or more short notes follow a dot they are played with dispatch, there being so many of them . . . short notes, when they precede dotted ones, are also played more rapidly than their notation indicates."

The double dot, although by no means unknown in Couperin's time, was not generally employed, probably because the simpler notation was easier to read and to write and the performance custom just described was universally accepted. Quantz tells us that "the time of the short notes after the dots cannot actually be fixed with complete exactness."

The French refer to this custom as *pointer*, overdotted.

The rhythm written:

should be played approximately:

An examination of his notation shows that we may be certain Couperin intended his compositions to be played *pointer*. His use of multiple flags on notes in the *Second Prelude* in measures 2, 13, 15 and 16 indicates clearly that the quick notes must be rushed in late. The realizations in light print on page 58 of the present volume illustrate the difficulties inherent in making an attempt to write a mathematically-correct notation of the overdotted performance. Although Couperin is sometimes inconsistent within a composition in the number of flags used, his intentions are always perfectly clear. The meticulous alignment of notes is further help in clarifying performance. The second measure of the *Seventh Prelude*, (see facsimile on page 9), for example, transcribed into treble and bass clefs, reads as follows:

The notation shows clearly that the bass A is played during the time of the dot beside F in the treble clef.

Throughout the Breitkopf and Härtel edition, the number of flags on quick notes has been altered, apparently to correct what looks like faulty arithmetic in the original edition. This has the invariable effect of distorting the performance by drastically altering the rhythm and, as in the case of the 2nd measure of the *Seventh Prelude*, altering the harmony as well. In the Breitkopf and Härtel edition, the measure is written as follows:

NOTES INEGALES INEQUALITY

The custom of playing certain stepwise successions of rhythmically uniform notes in an uneven rhythmic pattern was well established in the baroque era. Couperin was able to discuss it with one sentence having full confidence that the performer would know exactly what he meant. He wrote (page 49): " . . . we dot

Facsimile of the *Seventh Prelude*, measures 1-12
Reproduced by permission of the Bibliothèque Nationale

several eighth notes in succession moving by conjunct degrees; however, we write them in equal time values." The custom of playing with inequality is used by jazz musicians today, but the term "inequality" is archaic in their sphere. For example, the figure written:

is more likely to be performed, approximately:

This bending of the rhythm, limping, lilting or inequality, is a completely natural style of performance which is used in baroque music to add grace and elegance to the melody. There are two kinds of inequality: long-short and its reverse, short-long. In early manuscripts, long-short inequality is sometimes indicated by two-note slurs over stepwise successions of notes having the same time value. Couperin calls inequality in which the second note is longer than the first, *coulées* (sic). His notation for it is illustrated in the Table of Ornaments (#20) by a slur over pairs of notes in which the second note has a dot. Early French writers tell us that good taste alone determines whether the amount of inequality should be great or small, as different amounts change the expression considerably. For example, the progression written:

might be played with almost imperceptible inequality in the ratio of 4:3 or 3:4 :

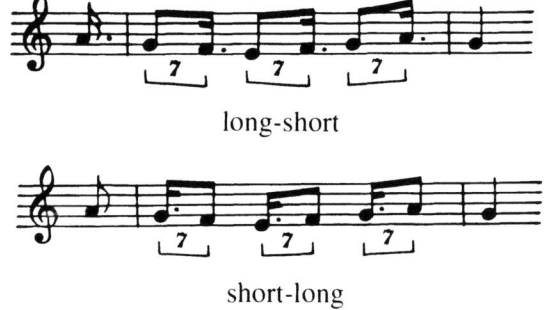

or with slightly more noticeable inequality in the ratio of 3:2 or 2:3:

long-short

short-long

or with very conspicuous inequality in the ratio of 2:1 or 1:2:

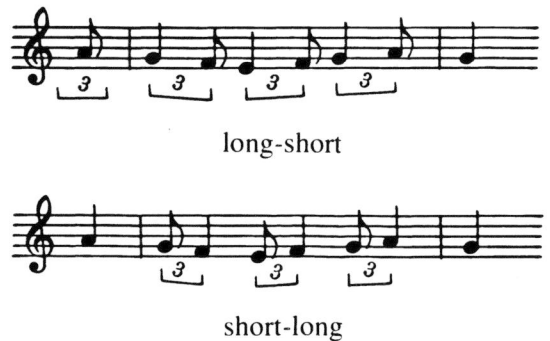

long-short

short-long

The examples show how much more difficult it is to write and read inequality than to play it.

Some of Couperin's fingerings seem to enforce the inequality indicated by the two-note slur. The combination of the two occurs in measure 15 of the *Second Prelude* (see the facsimile on page 6). The measure, which is written:

seems to indicate approximately the following interpretation:

There is a similar example of combined fingering and two-note slurs in measure 21 of the *Sixth Prelude*, page 68.

Although there are no two-note slurs, the fingering for both parts suggests inequality in measure 18 of the *Fourth Prelude* and in the upper part in measures 20 and 23 of the Fifth Prelude.

The legato indicated by a slur over more than two notes generally forbids inequality. In measure 16 of the *Second Prelude* inequality is required in the first half of the measure and forbidden by the long slur in the second half.

Other meanings of baroque slurs are discussed under *Fingering, Phrasing and Articulation* on pages 21-22.

Where there are no slurs, the use of inequality is left to the discretion of the performer, subject to certain rules with which he must become familiar. The following chart is a distillation of information gleaned from such writers as Loulié, Chocquel, Engrammel, D'Ilette, Montéclair and Corrette. The titles and dates of the works of these early French writers will be found in the bibliography on page 26.

WHERE INEQUALITY IS PERMITTED

These words require it: *inégales; notes inégales; lourer; pointer*.

- Groups of stepwise notes having shorter time value than the lower figure of the time signature

- Notes which fall naturally into pairs

- Melodies which become more elegant when played unequally

- Groups mainly uninterrupted by rests or notes of other time value

- Original slur over pairs of notes which are otherwise suitable

- A pickup note before a group played unequally adjusts to the inequality

WHERE INEQUALITY IS FORBIDDEN

These words forbid it: *également; notes égales; notes martelées; détachez; mouvement décidé; mouvement marqué; coups égaux*.

- Broken figures; passages with mainly leaping notes; repeated notes

- Triplets; syncopations; dotted notes

- Very fast tempi, which would sound frantic; very slow tempi, which would sound sluggish

- Mixed groups of notes and rests

- Original slur over more than two notes

- Original dots which look like staccatos forbid inequality

- Many authorities forbid inequality in Allemandes and in Marches. Some forbid it in accompaniment parts.

Facsimile from the *Premier Livre de Pièces de Clavecin* published in 1713
Reproduced by permission of the Syndics of the Fitzwilliam Museum, Cambridge

EXPLANATION OF ORNAMENTS AND SIGNS

ORNAMENTS WHICH BEGIN ON THEIR MAIN NOTE AND HAVE AUXILIARIES

Number in Table of Ornaments	Translation	Page in Text
1	Short mordent	34, 83
3	Long mordent	35
17	Mordents with sharps or flats	36
19	Continued mordent	39
24	Ascending slide of a third	39
26	Descending slide of a third	39
15	Accent	39

ORNAMENTS WHICH BEGIN ON AN AUXILIARY

Number in Table of Ornaments	Translation	Page in Text
6	Lower or ascending appoggiatura	37, 38
5	Lower appoggiatura and short mordent	37
7	Lower appoggiatura and long mordent	37
14	Detached trill	38, 39
9	Tied, stressed trill	39
12	Tied trill which is not stressed	39
10	Open trill	39
11	Closed trill	39
23	Continued trill	39
25	Turn	39

SIGNS WHICH MODIFY PERFORMANCE

Number in Table of Ornaments	Translation	Page in Text
13	Slurs. Signs for indicating that notes should be tied or slurred.	
20	Slurs in which the dot indicates that the second note of each beat should be dwelt upon.	49
16	Ascending arpeggio	39
18	Descending arpeggio	39
27	Aspiration	33, 34
29	Suspension	33, 34

OTHER SIGNS AND MISCELLANEOUS INFORMATION

4	Signs for repeating the refrain.	
8	Signs for holding the final notes.	
22	Signs for the end of the Rondos and their couplets.	
28	Unison. This bar indicates that when one finds the same note written in the right hand and in the left hand (which I suppose is a unison) one hand must play the note above the other.	
21	(N.B. The word *quarré* does not exist. This quaint and overlooked misprint should read *gravée*.) The lowest notes are never used except when harpsichords have been extended in their bass range. (The procedure called *ravalement*, in common use at the time, consisted of widening the harpsichord case to add additional keys at either end. Reference to *ravalement en hault*, at the upper end, will be found in the Sixth Prelude.)	
2	It is the value of the notes which must determine the duration of the mordents, the appoggiaturas and the trills. One must understand by the word 'duration' the greater or lesser number of repercussions or vibrations.	33

COUPERIN'S ORNAMENTATION

Although the custom of extemporizing ornaments during performance was well established by Couperin's time, he firmly repudiated it regarding his own compositions. Following the custom of his time, he included a Table of Ornaments and Signs in his first book of *Pièces*. He refers to it in *L'Art de toucher le Clavecin* and gives additional explanations for some of the ornaments he used. Nonetheless, custom dies hard, and in apparent anguish, he wrote in the Preface to the third book of *Pièces:*

> ". . . I am always surprised, after the pains I have given myself for marking the ornaments which are suitable to my Pièces (of which I have given, in part, a sufficiently clear explanation in a particular Method entitled L'Art de toucher le Clavecin) to hear persons who have learned them without heeding my instructions. This is an unpardonable negligence, the more so since it is not at all an arbitrary matter to put in what ornaments one wishes. I declare that in my pieces they ought to be played as I have marked them, and that they will never make a certain impression on persons of true taste, unless they have observed to the letter everything that I have marked, without adding or subtracting anything."

The general acceptance of Couperin's style of performing ornaments is borne out by the Tables of Ornaments of his contemporaries. The famous organist and composer D'Agincour, who had studied with Couperin, wrote in the Preface to his *Pièces de Clavecin* published in 1733:

> ". . . I would change nothing either in the ornaments or the method of playing them from that which M. Couperin has designated and characterized so well and which nearly all artists are using . . . It would be useless for me to give other explanations."

An understanding of Couperin's ornamentation is, therefore, absolutely essential to a correct performance of his works. Despite his vehemence, there are aspects of performing in which he allows great freedom to the performer. In other instances, his rules are very explicit. These have been summarized on page 25 for the convenience of the reader, as they are scattered through the book.

A facsimile of the Table of Ornaments is reproduced on pages 12 and 13. For the convenience of the modern performer, who should know both the French and English terminology of Couperin's ornaments, the Table has been translated and page numbers, where they are discussed in the text, have been included. Some of the ornaments in the Table are not discussed in *L'Art de toucher le Clavecin* and some variants which occur in the *Pièces* are in neither the Table nor the book. On pages 15-21, certain supplementary information is given in a discussion arranged according to the following classifications:

Ornaments which begin on their main note

Ornaments which begin on an auxiliary

Signs which modify performance and have no auxiliaries

Variants of the ornaments

Because he did not write the realizations in arithmetically-correct notation, new ones have been made which conform to our present day accuracy. Even so, it is not possible to capture on paper the freedom and style which are appropriate to each ornament in its particular context and these realizations must be considered functional rather than explicit.

In the following discussion, all numbers for ornaments refer to the Table on pages 12 and 13.

ORNAMENTS WHICH BEGIN ON THEIR MAIN NOTE AND HAVE AUXILIARIES

MORDENT, #1, 3, 17 and 19. The word mordent derives from *mordere*, to bite. The French writers use the term *pincé*, which Leopold Mozart describes as follows: "The mordent or the French *pincé* clings closely to the principal note, quietly and rapidly "bites," tweaks or pinches the same slightly and at once is released again." In the new engraving of the present volume, Couperin's elegant symbol ✝ has been replaced with the more familiar modern sign: ✦

The short mordent has one repercussion. The main note is accented, played on the beat and quickly followed by the lower auxiliary, which is the scale note unless Couperin modifies it with an accidental. The main note is then immediately re-played and held for the balance of its time value.

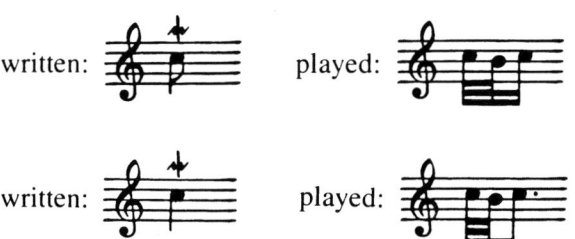

The long or double mordent has more repercussions. Couperin equates his use of it with the tremolo for string instruments. In example #3, there are three repercussions; in #7 and #17 there are two.

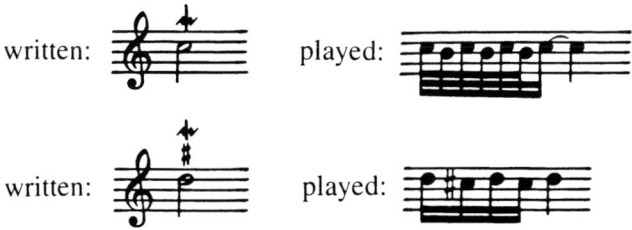

The repercussions of the continued mordent must stop before the entire time value of the main note has elapsed.

ASCENDING AND DESCENDING SLIDES OF A THIRD. #24 and #26. These ornaments are not discussed in the text. The auxiliary is the unwritten scale tone between the two main notes. The angle of the oblique line indicates the direction of the slide. It begins on the beat and is played quickly and gracefully. Slides are often incorporated into full chords; the passing dissonance adds great richness to the sound.

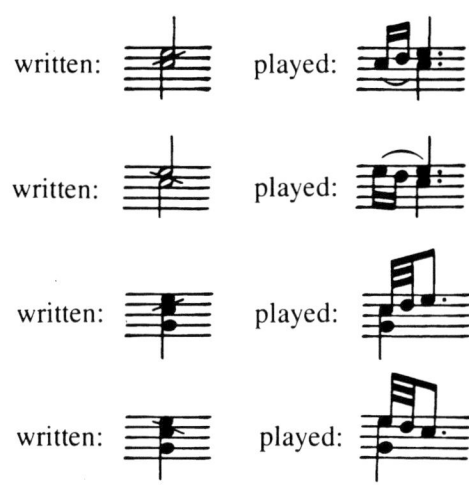

ACCENT, #15. The accent, a small note with no time value of its own, follows and is slurred from its main note. Often, it is an anticipation of the next note, but Couperin does not restrict it to that context. The accent has been called sigh, springer and aspiration by other early composers. (Couperin, however, reserves the term aspiration for a quite different effect; see #27.) In the Table, the accent takes one-fourth the time value of its main note but the nature of the ornament is such that its time value must be somewhat flexible.

Le Gazoüillement, VI, #3,
measure 24;

written:

Les Fastes, Acte IV, XI, #9,
measures 33-34;

written:

played:

ORNAMENTS WHICH BEGIN ON AN AUXILIARY

APPOGGIATURA, #6. The *port-de-voix* is a lower and the *coulé* an upper appoggiatura. The word derives from *appoggiare*, to lean. The appoggiatura is usually conjunct with its main note and dissonant with the bass. Since the dissonance is one of its most important features, the appoggiatura must be played on the beat, accented and slurred softly to the main note, which resolves the dissonance. Appoggiaturas are frequently used to connect main notes smoothly. One of the problems of interpretation in Couperin's ornamentation concerns the length of the appoggiatura. In example #6, it appears to take half the value of the main note. This agrees with the custom of the time which other writers describe in detail. It was also the custom to give the appoggiatura two-thirds of a main note having a dot beside it, but it is inherent in the nature of the ornament that it have some flexibility. There are instances throughout his keyboard works where a literal interpretation of these rules produces consecutive fourths or fifths. In other places, the physical aspect of measured performance seems to suggest a more flexible interpretation. This would be in agreement with the remarks on performing with good taste in *L'Art de toucher le Clavecin*. The performer, however, must judge each circumstance for himself and draw his own conclusions.

A discussion of the *Appoggiatura Between Descending Thirds* will be found on pages 19-20.

APPOGGIATURA AND SHORT MORDENT, #5.
APPOGGIATURA AND LONG MORDENT, #7.
In this combination of ornaments, each follows the rules given before. The mordent is played after the appoggiatura has taken its time from the main note.

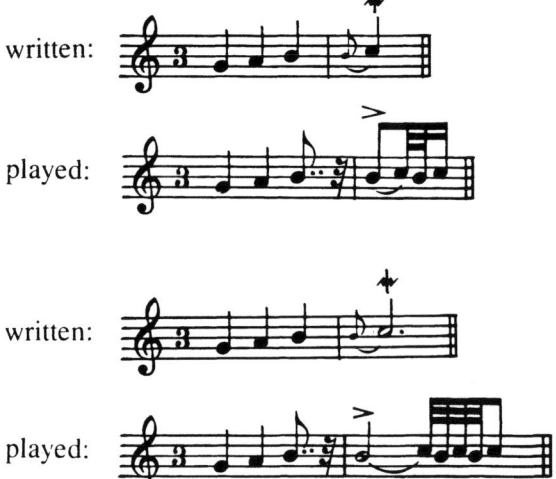

TRILL, #14, 9, 12, 10, 11, 23. Although there are six different types of trills in the Table, the same basic rules of performance apply to all. A trill is a more or less rapid alternation between the upper auxiliary and the main note. While the number of repercussions depends upon the performer's skill, all trills must have a minimum of four notes and must end on the main note. Other important information about performance style of trills will be found in the text. The differences among those in the Table are described on the following pages.

DETACHED TRILL, #14. The trill is shown in a context of descending seconds. It is not slurred either from the preceding or to the following note. There is no termination.

TIED TRILL WHICH IS DWELT UPON, #9. TIED TRILL WHICH IS NOT DWELT UPON, #12. The slur in these examples functions as a tie because the preceding note is the upper auxiliary of the trill. As a result, the repercussions of the trill do not begin until slightly after the beat of the main note. Montéclair says that the trill which is dwelt upon, *appuyé*, is begun by a long upper auxiliary. In #9 it is longer than the main note; in #12, both are the same length. The stopping point, shown in the realizations below, may be observed or not, according to context.

OPEN TRILL, #10, CLOSED TRILL, #11. The open trill occurs in an ascending and the closed trill in a descending progression. The trill is slurred to two 16ths written in full size notation, referred to as a termination or afterbeat. After the termination, the open trill is resolved by an ascending second and the closed trill by a descending second. In all other respects the trills are alike and the same interpretation is appropriate to both. In the realizations below, a) illustrates the point of view held by some authorities that the stopping point or *point d'arrêt* is required to make it clear to the ear that the terminal notes have time value of their own. In b), the termination is incorporated smoothly into the body of the trill and played at exactly same speed as the repercussions. In c), the first note of the trill is prolonged, one of the possible interpretations suggested by Couperin's text on pages 38 and 39.

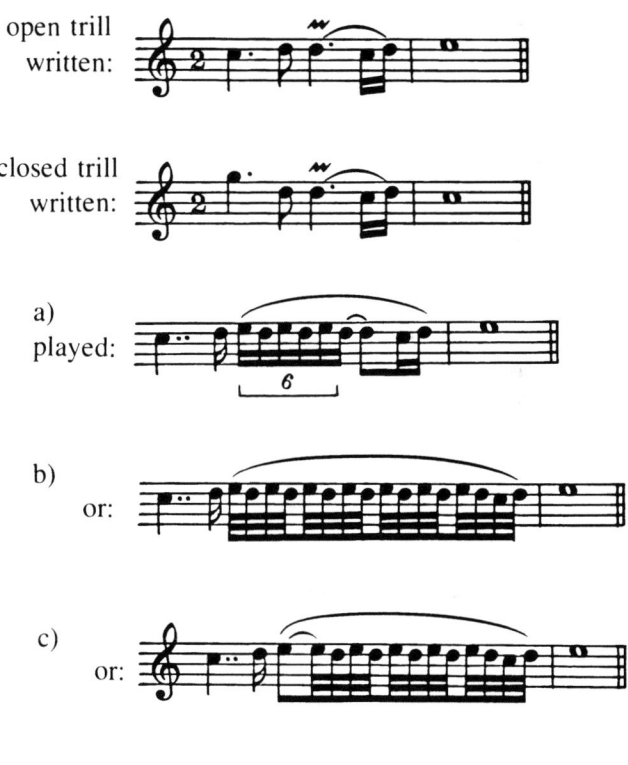

CONTINUED TRILL, #23. This trill is adjusted to suit its context, following the rules given for other trills and Couperin's suggestions on pages 38 and 39.

TURN #25. The turn is a four-note ornament with two auxiliaries. When placed directly above its main note, it begins on the beat and the notes are played in the following order: upper auxiliary, main note, lower auxiliary, main note. Couperin divides the time equally among the four notes, spreading them to fill the entire time of the main note. The notes are slurred.

SIGNS WHICH MODIFY PERFORMANCE AND HAVE NO AUXILIARIES

SLURS, #13. Couperin's slur is straight instead of curved. It is rendered as a modern curved slur in the new engraving of the present volume because its interpretation does not differ from modern practice. Frequently, a straight diagonal line appears between notes. One of the conventions of baroque performance practice was to articulate wide skips, and it often appears to be an indication not to articulate in those particular places.

The special meaning of slurred pairs of notes in conjunct succession is discussed on pages 8-11, *Inequality*.

COULÉES (SIC), NOTES SLURRED IN PAIRS IN WHICH THE SECOND NOTE ALSO HAS A DOT, #20. This notation for short-long inequality is discussed under *Inequality* on pages 8-11.

ASCENDING ARPEGGIO #16. DESCENDING ARPEGGIO #18. The conventional wavy line before a chord to indicate arpeggiation is hooked at the bottom for an ascending arpeggio and at the top for the descending. The first note of the arpeggiated chord is always played on the beat, the remaining ones played quickly, collected under the hand and held for the balance of the time value of the main notes.

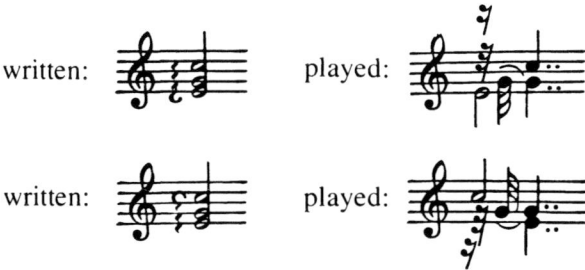

ASPIRATION, #27, SUSPENSION #29. Aspiration refers to a very small silence of articulation after a note; suspension refers to a very small silence of articulation before a note. Their use and effect are described in some detail in the text on page 33-4.

VARIANTS OF THE ORNAMENTS

Couperin frequently uses ornaments in quite different ways from those shown in the Table. Usually, the interpretation can readily be inferred from the Table or from the instructions in the text of *L'Art de toucher le Clavecin*. The principal ones, to which we refer here as variants of the ornaments, are the following:

1. The turn used between notes, either within the measure or across the bar line.
2. The slide incorporated into a chord; the slide on the interval of a fourth or a sixth.
3. Termination of a trill written in small notes having no time value. It is the opinion of many authorities that this is a trill without a stopping point. The termination is assimilated into the trill at the speed of the last repercussions played.

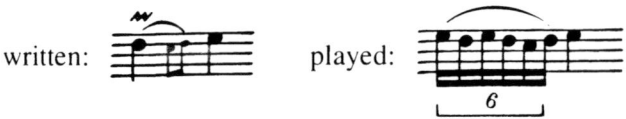

4. Combination of a trill and turn. Many authorities, including Dolmetsch, believe this to be another way of writing #3 above. Other authorities agree with the

interpretation given by Foucquet; that of a trill with stopping point followed by a full turn. Since Couperin does not discuss the ornament, the performer must decide for himself which interpretation to use.

5. Clusters of small notes with no time value appear without any apparent restriction. They are sometimes slurred as multiple-note appoggiaturas, that is, to the following main note. Sometimes they are slurred from the preceding main note, like multiple-note accents. Sometimes they enclose a main note from both sides.

An example of various types of clusters occurs in *La Rafraichissante*, IX, #2, measures 54-55.

Scale-like clusters occur fairly often. Measure 6 of the *Fifth Prelude* has the following:

THE APPOGGIATURA BETWEEN DESCENDING THIRDS

It has become common among writers and performers in recent years to regard the appoggiatura between descending thirds, in certain contexts, as an ornament which looks like an ordinary appoggiatura but behaves differently. Usually referred to as a *passing appoggiatura*, it is performed without accent in the time of the preceding note instead of its own main note which follows. The difference between the sounds of the two interpretations is quite striking.

Couperin's rule on page 38 is by no means without precedent. He wrote: "It is necessary for the little lost note of the lower appoggiatura or of an upper appoggiatura to be struck with the harmony; that is to say, during the time value of the (main) note which follows." Gaspard le Roux and d'Angelbert refer to the descending appoggiatura as a *port de voix descendant*, that is, an ascending appoggiatura which descends instead. Foucquet seems to be the only French writer who actually includes a written example in his *Method for Interpreting Ornaments*, where it appears as follows:

written:

played:

Boyvin, the early French writer who specifically advocated giving the appoggiatura a very short time value, wrote: "The *port de voix* is marked thus: +. It is necessary to make a short blow where it occurs, which is ordinarily descending. One must deaden this note, that is to say, not to hold it very long, but one must strike it directly with the bass." Rousseau illustrated the "passing" interpretation in his famous *Dictionnaire*, but on other extant tables of ornaments the descending appoggiatura is illustrated between seconds and fourths but not thirds. While the absence of an example may not be taken as positive proof that all descending appoggiaturas were regarded in the same manner, neither may it be taken as positive evidence of the opposite conclusion.

German writers who clearly describe the passing appoggiatura include Marpurg, J.J. Quantz, Leopold Mozart and C.P.E. Bach. Marpurg says the hooks on the notes must be reversed when the passing interpretation is called for. Otherwise, he makes the point that "all appoggiaturas in whatever progression they occur must fall exactly on the beat."

In Chapter VIII of his *Essay on Playing the Flute*, Quantz refers to the ancient French lineage of the passing interpretation of the appoggiatura and provides examples of correct and incorrect performance. He makes the further point that there is no difference whatever in the manner of notation. In seldom quoted passages in Chapter XIII, sections 30, 42, and 43, he also assigns the passing interpretation to certain ascending or descending seconds or leaps of fourths.

In Chapter 9, section 18 of *A Treatise on the Fundamental Principles of Violin Playing*, Leopold Mozart gives an example of correct performance of the passing appoggiatura which is similar to Quantz', but he also states that "the passing appoggiatura can also be used with notes which ascend or descend by conjunct degrees," and gives examples.

C.P.E. Bach, in his *Essay on the True Art of Playing Keyboard Instruments*, also describes the passing appoggiatura but castigates it as ugly and hateful.

The lack of a definite rule in *L'Art de toucher le Clavecin* defining the proper length for an appoggiatura seems to indicate that it had an inherent flexibility based on its context and governed by the performer's good taste. Whatever objections may be raised to consecutive fifths or octaves, which some use as the basis for the passing interpretation of the descending appoggiatura, is easily mitigated by playing them quite short. We have no evidence that Couperin (or his contemporaries) considered consecutives objectionable, in view of the fact that they sometimes occur in main notes.

There is, however, no possibility of proving that Couperin himself did or did not perform certain appoggiaturas in the passing manner, in view of the two positive instances in which he wrote them unmistakeably in the time of the preceding beat.

In Book I, the Fourth *Ordre*; the second part of *Les Bacchanales*, entitled *Tendresses Bacchiques* has the following in measures 20-22 and 33. The apparently unavoidable interpretation is that of a passing appoggiatura in the lower line, on a descending second.

In Book 2, the Ninth *Ordre*, *La Séduisante*, the appoggiatura in measure 12 is written in the preceding measure and tied as well as slurred across the bar line to an ascending fourth.

The original edition is not crowded in either case, therefore, a lack of space did not occasion the placement of the appoggiaturas in the preceding measures. It gives rise to the unanswerable question: Does the fact that Couperin himself did write appoggiaturas in the passing style indicate that he wrote the exception to his own practice in such a way that it prevented any misinterpretation? Or does it signify that, despite his comment on page 38 (quoted before), he did, nonetheless, expect some of his appoggiaturas to be performed as passing ornaments?

If the answer to the second question is "yes," in the performer's opinion, then he is faced with another question as well. Are passing appoggiaturas in Couperin's music confined to descending thirds in certain contexts, or they admissable in other places where the progression ascends in seconds or fourths or descends in seconds? For example, how is measure 5 in the Second Prelude to be played? (p. 58)

L'Art de toucher le Clavecin is a textbook on performance and style. For this reason, the realizations in light print in the present edition are written in accordance with Couperin's stated rules. The performer must judge the merits of each occurrence separately in order to formulate his own opinion of how best to perform them.

FINGERING, PHRASING AND ARTICULATION

In the baroque era, good phrasing, articulation and fingering were so totally interwoven that to have one without the others was impossible. Modern keyboard fingering, which provides for many considerations unrelated to specific phrasing and articulation, is different in both its point of view and its practical application. For this reason, careful study of Couperin's fingering is necessary in arriving at an interpretation which is consistent with the principles of phrasing and articulation he followed.

The shape of the hand and the natural strengths and weaknesses of the fingers are taken into consideration in deciding the best fingering. It is assumed that adjacent fingers are used on adjacent keys unless otherwise indicated. The fingering for ornamented notes is, without exception, for the main note. All the important differences between Couperin's fingering and modern systems are illustrated in *L'Art de toucher le Clavecin*. A brief discussion of them follows, and the page references will enable the reader to put the examples into context quickly.

LATERAL SHIFT OF THE HAND. These shifts are as positive an indication of phrasing as slur signs. (*Les Silvains*, 2nd quoted example, p. 52)

ADJACENT NOTES PLAYED WITH THE SAME FINGER. Legato is sometimes secured by sliding from a raised to a natural key with the same finger, (*Les Charmes*, p. 81.) Articulation is sometimes produced by playing consecutive, adjacent natural keys with the same finger (*Les Silvains*, p. 51.)

ASPIRATION AND SUSPENSION. Both are indications for articulations. His detailed discussion of their use as expressive ornaments emphasizes the fact that one of the chief means of making Couperin's music expressive is good articulation. Both are used on plain and on ornamented notes. (*Ondes*, 3rd couplet, p. 54.)

USE OF THE THUMB. Couperin uses the thumb freely but rarely passes it under the hand. The lack of long, legato, scalewise passages eliminates the need for thumb technic as it exists in modern music. A typical example of use of the thumb as a pivot in the left hand occurs in the last example from *L'Atalante*, p. 83.

FINGER SUBSTITUTION. Couperin uses this technic to secure legato where the range of the passage exceeds finger extension. It also occurs in places where a wide interval would otherwise be articulated according to the prevailing customs of the time. (*La Milordine*, p. 51.) Overlapping harmonies, one of several ways of enhancing the resonance of the harpsichord, are also produced by substitution. (*First Prelude*, measures 2-3, p. 56.)

SLURS. The wealth of slurs in Couperin's music is truly remarkable in an eighteenth century edition, and the slurs which cross bar lines are almost without precedent. (La Villers, p. 53.) Slurs are used in all possible contexts. They occur from strong to weak beats and the reverse. (*Evolutions:* Progression of thirds for left hand, p. 44.) The use of slurs to enforce or preclude inequality is discussed on pages 8-11 of the present volume. One of the traditions of baroque performance was the use of 'ordinary movement' which was somewhat articulate. It applies to many types of compositions and it frequently appears that Couperin used slurs to indicate that which should be played somewhat articulately and that which should be played legato.

UNUSUAL FINGER CROSSINGS AND TWO-NOTE SLURS: Very short phrases, characteristic of much baroque music, are well exemplified in scalewise progressions. Fingerings which are uncommon today facilitate this type of phrasing and are well suited to the action of the harpsichord.

> Right hand ascending: 3-4-3-4 *Les Ondes,* 4th couplet, p. 55.
> Left hand descending: 3-4-3-4 *La Triomphante,* top of p. 82.
> Right hand descending: 3-2-3-2 *Les Ondes,* 4th couplet, p. 55, last measure.

Further discussion of these fingerings and the two-note slur which sometimes accompanies them will be found on pages 8-11 of the present volume under *Inequality.*

DIAGONAL LINES BETWEEN NOTES. Couperin uses them as a further way of indicating legato connection of notes which otherwise would likely be articulated. (*Seventh Prelude* measures 10-11, p. 72.)

SLURS USED WITH APPOGGIATURAS AND ACCENTS. The slur between an appoggiatura and its main note or between a main note and its accent is missing in Couperin's music only in very rare instances which appear to be engraving errors. Other early writers specifically describe the very brief silence of articulation, taken from the preceding note, which should always be observed before appoggiaturas. This almost imperceptible silence serves to accent the dissonance of the appoggiatura, which is then slurred softly to its main note. A similar silence should also follow an accent in order to enhance its effect.

SLUR SIGNS DISCONTINUED WHERE A PATTERN IS ESTABLISHED. Where a consistent pattern of phrasing was obvious, early composers frequently indicated only the first few phrase groups. An example of Couperin's use of this custom occurs in measures 9 & 10 of *Le Moucheron* (p. 77). In the original edition, there are slurs for the first three groups of notes, as follows:

Although he did not write the slurs in the example in *L'Art de toucher le Clavecin,* the fingering clearly indicates that the phrasing should be continued as follows:

COUPERIN'S DEFINITION OF PHRASING. Couperin provided additional indications for correct phrasing in his third and fourth books of *Pièces de Clavecin.* He explains in the Preface to the third book:

> "One will find a new sign which looks like this figure: ❜ It is to indicate an end of the melody or our harmonic phrases and to make it clear that it is necessary to separate the end of the melody a little before passing on to what follows. In general, this is nearly imperceptible, but when one does not observe this little silence, persons of taste and feeling will feel that something is lacking in the execution; in a word, it is the difference between those who read everything straight through and those who pause at periods and commas. These silences must make themselves felt without altering the beat."

The phrasing commas delineate groups ranging in length from one-half to five and a half measures. A few fingerings and phrasing commas have been added in light print in the new engraving of the present volume. Although it is not possible to perform any of Couperin's *Pièces* or *Preludes* without some phrasing and articulation, if due attention is given to all of his carefully written directions, the modern performer may find the additional suggestions helpful. He should never feel obliged to use them, however, as his own persuasion of style must be followed.

EXPRESSION AND STYLE

Couperin expressed the ideal of good taste and style in the Preface to the first book of *Pièces de Clavecin*. He wrote:

> "Experience has taught me that hands that are strong and capable of executing that which is fastest and lightest are not always those which succeed best in the tender and sentimental pieces, and I would acknowledge in good faith that I like better what touches me than what surprises me.
>
> The harpsichord is perfect when its sound is spread out and is brilliant by itself, but as it is not able to swell or diminish its sounds, I would always gain greater pleasure from those who, by their art sustained by infinitely good taste, render this instrument susceptible of expression."

The term "light and shade" is used by other early writers to describe the expressive effects of increasing and diminishing sounds, and part of the meaning of good taste is the ability to communicate nuances of phrasing and expression. The English organist-composer Charles Avison wrote an entire book on the subject. The following passages are quoted from his *Essay on Musical Expression* (London, 1753):

> ". . . the judicious Performer, by this Exertion of his *Fort* or Master-Style, may possibly give a pleasing Tenderness or Spirit, even to an indifferent Composition; while on the other Hand, a Neglect, or Ignorance, of the Use of this Art, however expert in other Respects the Performer may be, will disguise, if not intirly (sic) destroy, those distinguished Beauties, which alone can raise the Dignity and Perfection of Music . . ."

> ". . . it will naturally occur to him [the Reader] how commanding the Power of Expression may be found, from a different Manner of reading the same Author; especially in Poetry, where a just and spirited Emphasis is so highly essential to point out those interesting Strokes, which are more peculiarly designed to delight the Imagination and affect the Heart. But how infinitely short of this Design, is the best wrote Poem, whether we hear it rehearsed with wild and vehement Accents, or repeated in a cold and lifeless *Monotone*? In either of these Cases, our Disgust, or Weariness of Attention, will be found in Proportion to the Beauties of the Author so abused. And just thus it fares with an injudicious Performance of a fine musical Composition."

> ". . . It is supposed, by many, that a real good Taste cannot possibly be acquired by any Rules of Art; it being a peculiar Gift of Nature, indulged only to those who have naturally a good Ear: and, as most flatter themselves that they have this Perfection, hence it happens, that he who sings or plays, thinks of nothing so much as to make continually some favourite Passages or Graces, believing that by this Means he shall be thought to be a good Performer, not perceiving that playing in good Taste doth not consist of frequent Passages, but in expressing, with Strength and Delicacy, the Intention of the Composer."

THE PRELUDE. In the baroque era, a Prelude was often played while the audience settled down for the evening's entertainment. Many times it was improvised on the spot, but Couperin wrote his Eight Preludes in full for the performer who did not have the natural genius requisite for such improvisation. It is probable that performers played even the written Preludes from memory to help create the illusion of extemporaniety. Little virtuosities made the audience anxious to hear more from the brilliant performer.

Practically speaking, the Prelude gave the performer the opportunity to test the acoustics of the room and the resonance of the instrument. He used this information to establish the speed of the pieces to follow. Slow pieces were played a little faster than usual on an instrument with very short sustaining power and trills were played faster in a room with fairly dead acoustics, etc. During the Prelude the performer was also loosening his fingers, judging the action and tuning of the instrument and establishing the tonality of the key of the first piece he would perform.

RHYTHMIC LIBERTIES. Besides the liberties in applying the conventions of overdotting and inequality, described on pages 8-11, Couperin allows a certain freedom in the unmeasured Preludes which he describes on page 70. This freedom however, must never constitute distortion. No note should sound so much longer or shorter that it could have been written with a different time value.

TEMPO. The tempos suggested in light print for the Preludes are based on early traditions. Muffat says that Preludes in 2 time have two slowish beats to the bar; ₵ has two quickish beats to the bar; C has four slowish beats but should not be faster than andante. 3/8 and 6/8 are lighter and quicker than 3/4 and 6/4. The performer should feel free to select other tempos than those suggested.

PIANO OR HARPSICHORD? The title of Couperin's important treatise does not preclude playing his works on the piano. The word *clavecin* was as much an indication that the works were not particularly suitable for organ as it was a specific indication that they were not suitable for wind or string instruments. The pianoforte had not yet come into being. Couperin describes the attributes and deficiencies of the harpsichord (p. 46) and it is very possible that the ability of the piano to swell and diminish its sounds would have delighted him.

Although the harpsichord is a keyboard instrument, the operative mechanism is a jack fitted with a plectrum or "plucker." Downward movement of a key causes the jack to rise and the plectrum to pluck the string in passing; the sound is of limited duration and the specific volume of the plucked string can be varied by only minute amounts. Specific changes of volume are accomplished by additional registers, or sets of strings and jacks, which are engaged by draw knobs or knee levers. Modern harpsichords are often fitted with pedals which make it possible to change registers with lightning speed. On most early instruments, changes were made only at agogic pauses, caesuras, repeats or between sections. Harpsichord ornamentation was a direct outgrowth of the inherent capabilities of the instrument. As a result of the desire to produce more "light and shade" in harpsichord music, dynamic changes and nuances were built into the composition itself.

DYNAMICS. Couperin increases volume by adding voices, thus thickening the texture; by overlapping harmonies, increasing the resonance; by the repercussions of trills and mordents; by the passing dissonances of slides; by the "buzzing" effect of simultaneous ornaments. It was a performance custom to accent all dissonances and altered notes. Articulations make the next note seem louder.

He decreases volume by removing voices, thus thinning the texture; by supporting a melody with only the sketchiest harmony; by spreading the voices further apart.

Aspirations and suspensions produce great refinement of expression; overdotting produces exhilaration in some compositions, a feeling of majesty in others; inequality adds elegance or pathos.

PEDAL AND DYNAMICS ON THE PIANO. The damper pedal has no equivalent on the harpsichord. If used in Couperin's music, its effect must be an enhancement of the written-in effects and not a separate effect imposed on the music. The swell shadings possible on the piano should not be exaggerated.

François Couperin, called the Great

SUMMARY OF COUPERIN'S RULES

Regarding style and ornaments, Couperin stated some definite rules and indicated other places where a degree of flexibility is left to the performer. Some which can be found in *L'Art de toucher le Clavecin* are summarized briefly below. The page references may be used to place the remarks into correct context.

DEFINITE RULES

Ornaments
1. They must be very precise. — 70
2. Those made up of repercussions must be played evenly with an imperceptible speeding up. — 70
3. The Table of Ornaments in the first book of *Pièces* must be followed. — 39
4. The time value of the notes determines the duration of short and long mordents and of appoggiaturas followed by mordents. — 34
5. Mordents must begin and end on their main note. — 35
6. Mordents must have a stopping point. — 35
7. Trills must begin on the tone or semi-tone above the written note. — 38
8. Trills begin more slowly than they end; the acceleration must be imperceptible. — 38
9. Trills of any considerable length have a stopping point. — 39
10. The little note of an ascending or a descending appoggiatura must be struck with the harmony, that is to say, in the time of the main note which follows. — 38

Fingering:
1. Fingering does much for good playing; certain fingering produces certain effects. — 31
2. Use your own better fingers for playing trills and appoggiaturas. — 32, 38
3. Consecutive, conjunct notes may be played with the same finger when the first is aspirated or when the second of them is played on the last part of the beat. — 54

Style:
1. Adhere strictly to the beat where the word *mesuré* is used. — 70
2. Do not alter the rhythm in the regulated pieces. — 70
3. Hold all notes for their full time value. — 70
4. Use today's good taste in playing. — 70
5. Don't play tender pieces as slowly as if they were being played on other instruments. — 50
6. Always play delicately on the harpsichord. — 30, 50
7. It is necessary to preserve a perfect legato in all that you play. — 70

FLEXIBILITY LEFT TO THE PERFORMER

Ornaments:
1. Trills, other than those of considerable length, may have stress on the upper note, may be so short they have no stress, may have no stopping point, may be played with a brief rest after them, depending on context. — 39
2. Detach the aspiration less quickly in slow and tender pieces than in the light and rapid ones. — 34
3. The length of silence before the suspension is governed by the good taste of the performer. — 34

Style:
1. Where the word *mesuré* is not used, the *Preludes* may be played without attaching too much precision to the notated rhythm. — 70
2. We dot several eighth notes in succession moving by conjunct degrees, however we write them in equal time values. — 49

BIBLIOGRAPHY

The principal works by other writers which are referred to in the Foreword of the present volume are listed below with the pages where the reference is made.

Agincour, D' *Premier Livre de pièces de Clavecin* (1733)	11, 14
Anglebert, D' *Premier Livre de pièces de Clavecin* (1689)	19
Avison, C. *An Essay on Musical Expression* (London, 1752)	23
Bach, C.P.E. *Essay on the True Art of Playing Keyboard Instruments* (Berlin, 1759)	8, 20
Boyvin, J. *Premier Livre d'Orgue* (1689)	20
Burney, C. *A General History of Music from the Earliest Ages to the Present Period* (London, 1776-89)	3
Corrette, M. *Nouveau Livre de Noëls pour le Clavecin ou l'Orgue Premier Livre de pièces de Clavecin* (1735)	10, 11
Dieupart *Six suittes de Clavessin* (ca. 1700-1710)	20
Dolmetsch, A. *The Interpretation of the Music of XVII and XVIII Centuries as Revealed by Contemporary Evidence* (London, 1916)	4, 7, 19
Engrammelle *La Tonotechnie, ou l'art de noter des cylindres* (Paris, 1775)	10, 11
Foucquet *Méthodes pour apprendre la manière de se servir des agrémens utiles à la propreté des pièces de Clavessin*	19
Le Roux, G. *Pièces de clavessin avec la manière de les joüer* (1705)	19
Loulié, E. *Elémens de la musique* (1696)	11, 20
Marpurg *Die Kunst das Clavier zu spielen* (Berlin, 1750) *Principes du Clavecin* (Berlin, 1756)	20
Montéclair *Principes de musique divisez en quatre parties* (1736)	10, 11, 17
Mozart, Leopold *A Treatise on the Fundamental Principles of Violin Playing* (Augsburg, 1787)	15, 20
Muffat, G. *Florilegium Primum* (Augsburg, 1695)	23
Quantz, J.J. *On Playing the Flute* (Berlin, 1752)	8, 20
Rameau, J-Ph. *Réimpression des Pièces de clavessin 1724 avec une table des agrémens* (1731)	20
Rousseau, J-J. *Dictionnaire de la Musique* (1768)	20

OTHER SUGGESTED BOOKS FOR READING

Anthony, J. *French Baroque Music from Beaujoyeulx to Rameau*
Brunold, P. *Traité des Signes et Agréments Employés par les Clavecinistes Français des XVIIe et XVIIIe Siècles*
Bukofzer, M. *Music in the Baroque Era*
Dannreuther, E. *Musical Ornamentation*
Dart, T. *The Interpretation of Music*
Donington, R. *The Interpretation of Early Music*
Dorian, F. *The History of Music in Performance*
Mellers, W. *François Couperin and the French Classical Tradition*

ACKNOWLEDGMENTS

I would like to express my appreciation to the Bibliothèque Nationale and the Syndics of the Fitzwilliam Museum for permission to publish facsimiles of early editions. I also want to thank Iris and Morton Manus of the Alfred Publishing Co. for the care with which they helped to prepare this edition and Judith Simon Linder for her valuable suggestions in the preparation of the manuscript. In particular I wish to thank Willard A. Palmer for his unfailing encouragement and valuable suggestions.

L'ART
DE TOUCHER LE CLAVECIN

PAR MONSIEUR COUPERIN,

Organiste du Roy. &c.

DEDIÉ

A SA MAJESTE

Gravé par L. Hüe   *Prix 6ᵗᵗ en blanc.*

A PARIS.

Chés
- *L'Auteur, au coin de la rüe des foureurs vis a vis les Carneaux.*
- *Le Sieur Foucaut, rüe Saint honnoré: à la Régle d'or. Proche la rüe des Bourdonnois.*

AVEC PRIVILEGE DU ROY.
1716.

Facsimile of the Title Page from the Original Edition of 1716
Reproduced by permission of the Bibliothèque Nationale

L'ART DE TOUCHER LE CLAVECIN

By FRANÇOIS COUPERIN

TRANSLATOR'S NOTE. The line between readability in English and faithful rendering of Couperin's quaint, courtly French, is sometimes hard to draw. In preparing the completely new English translation of the present volume, every effort has been made to preserve the very original personality that shines through his writing. The original French text has been included (without alteration of its archaic spellings and punctuations) because the translation of some terms and expressions necessarily involves some personal opinion and the reader of a technical treatise must be free to exercise his own judgements. Missing and incorrectly printed accents have not been altered. Some explanatory footnotes have been added to help clarify some fairly obscure sentences.

(a) PREFACE TO THE FIRST EDITION PUBLISHED IN 1716

PREFACE

La mèthode que je donne, est une espèce de restitution que je fais au public: ayant profité autant qu'il mà èté possible des bons ans qu'on à bien voulu me donner sur mon art. Je les ay joins à mes petites dècouvertes: ainsi, je serai trop content sy je puis m'acquiter sufisamment. Quelques pèrsonnes diront peut-ère qu'un dévoilant mes recherches particulieres je travaille contre mes propres interêts! mais je les sacrifierai toujours, sans aucune rèserve quand il s'agira de l'utilité des autres.

PREFACE

The method that I present here is a kind of restitution to the public, having profited as much as possible from the compliments they have so kindly given me concerning my art. I have added my little discoveries to this and thus I will feel that I have done enough in discharging my duty to them. Perhaps a few people will say that I work against my own best interests in these disclosures of my studies, but I will renounce them forever, without any reservations at all, whenever it is a matter of usefulness to others.

PREFACE TO THE SECOND EDITION PUBLISHED IN 1717

PREFACE

La Méthode que je donne icy est unique, et n'a nul raport à la Tablature, qui n'est qu'une sçience de Nombres; mais j'y traite sur toutes choses (par principes démontrés) du beau-Toucher du Clavecin. J'y crois même donner des Notions assés claires (du goût qui convient à cet instrument) pour être aprouvé des habiles, et aider ceux qui aspirent à le devenir. Comme il y a une grande distance de la Grammaire, à la Déclamation; il y en a aussi une infinie entre la Tablature, et la façon de bien-joüer. Je ne dois donc point craindre que les gens éclaircir s'y méprénent; je dois seulement exhorter les autres à la docilité, et à se dépoüiller des préventions qu'ils pouroiens avoir, au moins les dois-je assurer tous, que ces principeu sont absolument nécessaires pour parvenir à bien éxécuter mes Pièces.

PREFACE (b)

The method that I present here is unique, and has no connection with the tablature which is but the science (c) of numbers. Here I deal with all matters regarding fine harpsichord playing (by proven principles). I believe I have given sufficiently clear notions (on the style which is suited to this instrument) to be approved of by the skillful and to help those who aspire to become so. As there is a great distance from grammar to declamation, so there is an infinitely greater one between the tablature and good playing style. I do not have to fear, therefore, on this point, that those who are enlightened will be mistaken. I have only to exhort others to docility and to divest themselves of any prejudices they may have. At least, I have to assure everyone that these principles are absolutely necessary to succeed in playing my pieces well.

(a) See also the discussion of both original editions on pages 4 and 5.

(b) We can only speculate that some people had raised questions about Couperin's notation and fingering after the first edition had appeared, and that this occasioned the completely different Preface which seems designed to enlighten the unlearned without offending the erudite.

(c) Although some writers translate *tablature* as musical theory, it seems to be rather too general a term. Tablatures for lute and keyboard had been in use for a long time and consisted of a series of parallel lines, like a staff, on which the pitch of each note was indicated by numbers and/or letters. Rhythm was notated above this staff. The inability of some people to read his staff notation may have occasioned the remark.

PLAN DE CETTE METHODE

La position du corps, celle des mains, Les agrémens qui seruent au jeu, De petits exercises-preliminaires, et essentiels, pour paruenir à bien joüer, Quelques remarques sur la maniere de bien doigter; relatiues à beaucoup d'endroits de mes deux livres de Piéces. Huit préludes diversifiés, proportionnés au progrés que je Suppose qu'on doit faire; dont les doigts sont chiffrés; Et que j'ai entremèlés d'obseruations pour executer auec goust, sont les parties de cet ouvrage.

La modestie de quelques-uns des plus habiles Maitres de clavecin qui sans répugnance m'ont fait L'honneur à differentes fois de venir me consulter sur la maniere, Et le goust de toucher mes pieces me fait esperer que Paris, la Province, et les Etrangers, qui tous les ont reçües favorablement, me sçauront gré de leur donner une méthode sure, pour les bien executer; et même c'est ce qui ma dèterminé à la donner entre mon premier Livre de pieces et le second qui vient d'estre mis aujour.

Pour la facilité de ceux qui joüent les pieces de mes deux livres, j'expliqueray, et je chifreray les endroits les plus équivoques; et l'on poura tirer de ces exemples, des consequences utiles pour d'autres occasions.

L'âge propre à commencer Les enfans, est de six, à sept-ans: non pas que cela doive exclure Les personnes plus avancées: mais, naturèlement, pour mouler; et former des mains à L'exercise du Clavecin, le plutot, est le mieux; et comme la bonne-grace y est necessaire il faut commencer par la position du corps.

Pour être assis d'une bonne haulteur, il faut que le dessous des coudes, des poignets; et des doigts soit de niveau: ainsy on doit prendre une chaise qui s'accorde à cette régle.

On doit mettre quelque chose de plus, ou de moins hault sous les pieds des jeunes personnes, à mesure qu'elles croissent; afin que leurs pieds n'étant point en l'air, puissent Soûtenir le corps dans un juste équilibre.

PLAN OF THIS METHOD

These are the parts of this work: The position of the body, that of the hands, the ornaments which are used in playing, little preliminary exercises and essentials for succeeding in playing well, some remarks on the manner of good fingering related to many passages in my two books of pieces,(a) eight diversified Preludes proportioned to the progress that I assume one should make, in which the fingers are numbered; and I have interspersed observations for playing with taste.

The modesty of some more skillful masters of the harpsichord, who, without reluctance have at different times honored me by consulting me on style and good taste in playing my pieces, has made me hope that Paris, the Provinces and foreigners, who have received all of them favorably, will be grateful to me for giving them a reliable method for playing them well; and it is this which has made me determined to give this work between my first book of pieces and the second, which has just been published.(b)

To make it easier for those who play the pieces in my two books, I will give explanations and will finger the most ambiguous passages; and they can draw useful inferences from these examples for other occasions.

The appropriate age for young children to begin is six or seven years; not that that excludes persons of more advanced age: but naturally, to mold and form the hands by exercises at the harpsichord, the sooner the better; and, as good grace is necessary, one must begin with the position of the body.

In order to be seated at the correct height, the under side of the elbows, wrists and the fingers must be all on one level: so one must choose a chair which agrees with this rule.

It will be necessary to put something of suitable height under young people's feet, measured by their growth, so that their feet are not dangling in the air and so they can keep their bodies properly balanced.

(a) The edition of 1716 reads: . . . *de mon premier Livre* . . . 'in my first book.'

(b) The first edition reads . . . *à la donner auant mon Second Livre de pieces, quoy que jusse promis ce immediatement après Le premier* . . . 'before my Second Book of Pieces, which I had already promised immediately after the First.'

La Distance à laquelle une personne formée doit être du clavier est à peu prés de neuf-pouces, à prendre de la ceinture; et moindre à proportion pour les jeunes personnes.

Le milieu du corps, et celui du clavier doivent se raporter.

On doit tourner, un tant soit peu le corps sur la droite étant au clavecin: ne point avoir Les genoux trop serrés; et tenir ses pieds vis-à vis L'un de L'autre; mais Surtout le pièd droit bien en dehors.

A L'egard des grimaces du visage on peut S'en coriger soy-même en mettant un miroir Sur le pupittre de L'epinette, ou du clavecin.

Sy une personne a un poignet trop hault en jouant, le seul remède que j'aye trouvé, est de faire tenir une petite baguétte-pliante par quelqu'un; laquelle sera passée par dessus le poignet déffectueux: et en mêmetems par dessous L'autre poignet. Sy le déffaut est opposé, on fera le contraire. Il ne faut pas, avec cette baguette, contraindre absolument celuy, ou celle qui joüe. Petit-à-petit ce déffaut se corige; et cette invention m'a Seruie tres utilement.

Il est mieux, et plus séant de ne point marquer la mesure de la Teste, du corps, n'y des pieds. Il faut avoir un air aisé à Son clavecin: Sans fixer trop la vuë Sur quelque objet, ny L'auoir trop vague: enfin regarder La compagnie, s'il S'en trouve, comme Sy on n'étoit point occupé d'ailleurs. Cet avis n'est que pour ceux qui joüent Sans le Secours de Leurs Livres.

On ne doit Se Servir d'abord que d'une épinette, ou d'un seul clavier de clavecin pour la premiere jeunesse; et que L'une, ou L'autre Soient emplumés tres foiblement; cet article ètant d'une consequence infinie, La belle execution dèpendant beaucoup plus de la Souplesse, et de la grande Liberté des doigts, que de la force; en Sorte que dés Les commencemens Sy on Laisse jouer un enfant Sur deux claviers, il faut de toutte nècessité qu'il outre ses petites-mains pour faire parler les touches; et delá viennent les mains mal-placées, et la dureté du jeu.

The distance which an adult should be from the harpsichord is about nine thumb-lengths, measured from the waist; and less in proportion for younger people.

The middle of the body and that of the keyboard should correspond.

One should turn the body slightly to the right when at the harpsichord. Do not have the knees too tightly together; and hold the feet side by side but especially the right foot well out to the side.

With regard to making facial grimaces, it is possible to correct oneself by placing a mirror on the music rack of the spinet or harpsichord.

If a person has too high a wrist in playing, the only remedy I have found is to have someone hold a little flexible stick which is passed over the faulty wrist and, at the same time, under the other wrist. If the defect is the opposite, do the contrary. Do not absolutely restrain the wrists with this stick, or they cannot play. Little by little, the defect is corrected; and this invention is very useful.

It is better and more becoming not to mark time with the head, the body or the feet. One must have an air of ease at his harpsichord, without fixing his gaze too much on one object or looking too vague; in short, looking at the company in which he finds himself, as if not occupied otherwise. This advice is for those who play without the help of their books.

One must use a spinet or a single keyboard (a) at first for the very young, and the one or the other should be extremely lightly quilled; this point being of infinite importance. Beautiful playing depends a great deal more on suppleness and great freedom of the fingers rather than on force, so that if, at the beginning, one allows a child to play on two keyboards, he will of necessity strain his small hands to make the notes sound and from this will come badly placed hands and a hard touch.

(a) When the two manuals (keyboards) of a harpsichord are coupled so they play together, the action is usually considerably heavier than on a single manual.

La Douceur du Toucher dépend encore de tenir ses doigts le plus prés des touches qu'il est possible. Il est Sensé de croire, (L'experience àpart) qu'une main qui tombe de hault donne un coup plus Sec, que sy elle touchoit de prés; et que la plume tire un Son plus dur de la corde.

Il est mieux, pendant les premieres Leçons qu'on donne aux enfans de ne leur point recommander d'étudier en L'absence de la personne qui leur enseigne: Les petites personnes sont trop dissipées pour s'assujètir à tenir leurs mains dans la Scituation qu'on leur a prescrite: pour moy, dans les commencemens des enfans j'emporte par précaution la clef de L'instrument Sur lequel je leur montre, afin qu'en mon absense ils ne puissent pas déranger en un instant ce que j'ay bien Soigneusement posé en trois quarts d'heures.

Séparément des agrémens usités, comme les tremblemens, pincés, ports-de-voix &c j'ay toujours fait faire à mes éléves de petites évolutions des doigts, soit de passages, ou de batteries diversifiées à commencer par les plus Simples, et Sur les tons les plus naturels; et insensiblement je les ay menés jusqu'aux plus Legers, et aux plus transposés; ces petits Exercises qu'on ne sçauroit trop multiplier, Sont autant, de matéreaux, tout prets à mettre en place; et qui peuvent Servir dans beaucoup d'occasions. J'en donneray quelques modéles àla Suite des agrémens cy-aprés, Sur Lesquels on en poura imaginer d'autres.

Les personnes qui commencent tard, ou qui ont été mal-montrées feront attention que comme les nerfs peuvent être endurcis, ou peuvent avoir pris de mauvais plis, elles doivent Se dénoüer, ou se faire dénoüer Les doigts par quelqu'un, avant que de Se méttre au clavecin; c'est adire Se tirer, ou Se faire, tirer Les doigts de tous les Sens; cela met d'ailleurs les Espirts en mouvement; et l'on Se trouve plus de liberté.

La façon de doigter sert beaucoup pour bien joüer: mais, comme il faudroit un volume entier de remarques, es de passages variés pour démontrer ce que je pense; et ce que Je fais pratiquer a mes éléves, je n'en donneray icy qu'une notion generale. Il est sûr qu'un certain chant, qu'un certain passage étant fait d'une certaine façon, produit à L'oreille, de la perssonne de goût, un éffet different.

Sweetness of touch depends, moreover, on holding the fingers as closely as possible to the keys. It is sensible to believe (apart from experience) that a hand which falls from a height will give a drier blow than if it plays from nearby; and that the quill will draw a harsher sound from the string.

It is better, during the first lessons given to children, not to recommend practice in the absence of the person who teaches them. Little people are too inattentive to subject themselves to holding their hands in the position which is stipulated for them. For myself, in the beginning lessons for children, as a precaution I carry the key to the instrument on which I teach them, so that in my absence they cannot undo in an instant that which I taught them so carefully in three quarters of an hour.

Apart from the ornaments used, like trills, mordents, appoggiaturas, etc., I always make my pupils play little finger exercises, either diversified passages or bateries [broken chords or arpeggios] beginning with the simplest and on the most natural tones and gradually leading them to the fastest and most transposed ones. These little exercises cannot be too multiplied; they are like so many supports ready to be put into place and will serve on many occasions. I shall give several models later, following the ornaments, upon which one will be able to devise others.

Those persons who begin late or who have been badly taught, will need attention, as the muscles will perhaps be hardened, or perhaps they have acquired bad habits. Before sitting down at the harpsichord, they should loosen or have their fingers loosened by someone; that is to say, to pull or to have someone pull their fingers in all directions, so that besides an understanding of movement, they will have greater freedom of movement.

The manner of fingering does much for good playing: but, as it would require a volume filled with remarks and varied passages to illustrate what I think and what I make my pupils practice, I will give only a general idea here. It is certain that a certain song played in a certain style of fingering will produce a different effect upon the ear of a person of taste. (a)

(a) Good fingering and good phrasing were inseparable in baroque music, as a study of Couperin's illustrative passages from his *Pièces* reveals. See pages 21 and 22 in this volume.

REFLEXION

Beaucoup de personnes ont moins de disposition à faire des tremblemens, et des port-de-voix de certains doigts: dans ce cas je conseille de ne point négliger de les rendre meilleurs en les exerçant beaucoup, mais, comme en mêmetems les meilleurs doigts se perfectionent aussy, il faut s'en servir par prèférence aux moindres, sans aucun ègard à L'ancien usage de doigter, qu'il faut quiter, en faveur de bien-joüer d'aujourd'huy.

AUTRE REFLEXION

On devroit ne commencer à montrer la tablature aux enfans qu'aprés qu'ils ont une certaine quantité de pieces dans les mains. Il est presqu'impossible, qu'en regardant leur Livre, les doigts ne ses dérangent; et ne se contorsionnent: que Les agrémens même n'en soient altèrés; d'ailleurs, La memoire se forme beaucoup mieux en aprenant par-coeur.

AUTRE REFLEXION

Les hommes qui veulent ariver à un certain degré de perfection ne devroient jamais faire aucun exercice pénible de leurs mains. Celles des femmes, par La raison contraire, sont généralement meilleures. J'ai dèja dit, que la souplesse des nerfs contribuë beaucoup plus, au bien-joüer, que la force; ma preüve est Sensible dans la différence des mains des femmes, à celles des hommes; et de plus, La main gauche des hommes, dont ils se servent moins dans les exercices, est communément las plus souple au clavecin.

DERNIERE REFLEXION

Je crois qu'on n'a pas douté en Lisant jusqu'ici, que ja n'aye supposé, qu'on a dû enseigner d'abord aux enfans, Le nom des notes du clavier.

REFLECTION

Many people have less aptitude for playing trills and appoggiaturas with certain fingers: in these cases, I advise them not to neglect to try to improve them by many exercises. But, at the same time, as the better fingers become more perfect, they should be used in preference to the weaker ones without any regard for the old style of fingering, which must be given up in favor of the good playing expected today.

ANOTHER REFLECTION

One should not begin to teach notation to children until after they have a certain number of pieces in their hands. It is next to impossible, while watching their book, for their fingers not to become disarranged and twisted; the ornaments themselves might even become changed; moreover, memory is formed much better in learning by heart.

ANOTHER REFLECTION

Men who wish to attain a certain degree of perfection should never do any rough work with their hands. Women's hands, on the contrary, are generally better. I have already said that the suppleness of the muscles contributes more to good playing than force. My proof is reasonable, in the difference in the hands of women from those of men, and furthermore, the left hand of men, which is used less in working, is commonly the more supple at the harpsichord.

LAST REFLECTION

I believe that there is no doubt, having read this far, that I have assumed that, anyone teaching children will teach them first the names of the notes of the keyboard.

PETITE DISSERTATION, SUR LA MANIERE DE DOIGTER, POUR PARVENIR A L'INTELLIGENCE DES AGREMENS QU'ON VA TROUVER.

J'ètablis par raport à cette méthode, (séparément de mon usage) qu'on commencera par compter La poulce, de chaque main, pour Le premier-doigt; en sorte que les chiffres iront ainsi.

main gauche   main droite
5.4.3.2.1.   1.2.3.4.5.

Cette intelligence servira pour les renvois de beaucoup d'endroits de mes pieces (équivoques pour les doigts) que je tâche d'èclaircir. On connoîtra par La pratique, combien le changement d'un doigt, à un autre, sur la même note, sera utile; et quelle liaison cela donne au jeu.

Les sons du clavecin étant décidés, chacun en particulier; et par consequent ne pouvant être enflés ny diminués: il à paru presqu'insoutenable, jusqu'à présent, qu'on put donner le L'amê à cèt instrument: cependant, par les recherches dont j'ay appuyé le peu de naturel que le ciel ma donné, je vais tâcher de faire comprendre par quelles raisons jay sçu acquerir Le bonheur de toucher Les personnes de goût qui m'ont fait L'honneur de m'entendre; et de former des éléues qui peutestre, me Surpassent. L'impression-sensible que je propose, doit son éffet à La cèssation; et à la suspension des sons, faites à propos; et selon les caractères qu'èxigent les chants des préludes, et des pièces. Ces deux agrémens par leur opposition, Laissent L'oreille indèterminée: en sorte que dans Les occasions ou les instrumens à archet enflent leurs sons, La Suspension de ceux du clavecin semble, (par un éffet contraire) retracer à L'oreille La chose souhaitée.

J'ay dèja expliqué, par des valeurs de notes, et par des silences, L'aspiration, et la suspension, dans La table des agrémens qui est à la fin de mon premier Livre: mais, j'éspere que L'idée que j'en viens de donner (quoy que succinte) ne sera pas inutile aux personnes susceptibles de sentiment.

A LITTLE ESSAY ON THE STYLE OF FINGERING FOR REACHING AN UNDERSTANDING OF THE ORNAMENTS WHICH WILL BE FOUND LATER.

Regarding this method (departing from my usual custom), I have decided to begin by counting the thumb on each hand as "1," for the first finger, so that the numbers will be as follows: (a)

Left Hand   Right Hand
5.4.3.2.1.   1.2.3.4.5.

This information will be useful frequently in returning to passages in my pieces (where the fingering seems ambiguous), that I will try to make clear. One can be a good judge through practice, of how useful it is, and what legato it gives to the playing, to change from one finger to another on the same note.

The sounds of the harpsichord have each been specifically determined and consequently cannot be increased or decreased. It has seemed almost impossible, up to the present, for anyone to give soul or feeling to this instrument. However, from the studies I have dwelt on and the little talent heaven has granted me, I will strive to make clear those reasons by which I have had the happiness of touching persons of good taste who have honored me by listening to me, and of training pupils who, perhaps, surpass me. This feeling that I suggest, owes its effect to the cessation and the suspension of tones, made opportunely and according to the character of the melody of the songs and preludes and pieces. These two ornaments, by their contrast, leave the ear undetermined in such a way that, in those places where the bowed instruments would increase their tone, the suspension at the harpsichord, by a contrary effect, seems to produce this desired result.

I have already explained in note values and rests, in the Table of Ornaments which is at the end of my first book, the aspiration and suspension; but I hope that the ideas that I am going to give (although succinct) will not be useless to those who are susceptible of feeling.

(a) Various systems for indicating fingering had been devised and used without regard for uniformity. It is possible that the system he had customarily used, referred to in this passage, was one in which the left hand little finger was numbered '1,' the thumb '5,' the right thumb '1' and the little finger '5.'

(b) See the discussion on page 24.

(c) The Table of Ornaments is reproduced in facsimile and translated on pages 12-13 of this volume.

Ces deux noms (d'aspiration, et de suspension) auront, sans doute, paru nouveaux: mais, au moins si quelqu'un se vante d'avoir pratiqué L'une, et L'autre, je ne crois pas qu'on me sçache mauvais gré, en general, d'avoir rompu La glace, en appropriant à ces deux sortes d'agrémens des noms qui conviennent à Leurs èffets; d'ailleurs j'ay jugé qu'il ètoit mieux de s'entendre Les uns, et les autres dans un art aussi estimé, et aussi pratiqué qu'est celuy de toucher le clavecin.

Quant à L'èffet-sensible de L'aspiration il faut détacher la note, Sur laquelle elle est posée, moins vivement dans les choses tendres, et lentes, que dans celles qui sont lègères, et rapides.

A L'ègard de la suspension! elle n'est gueres usitée que dans les morceaux tendres, et lents. Le silence qui précéde la note sur laquelle elle est marquée doit être réglé par le goût de la personne qui èxècute.

These two names (aspiration and suspension) will doubtless seem novel, but at least if anyone boasts of having used one or the other, I don't believe anybody will be annoyed with me, generally, to have broken the ice in appropriating these names which are so suited to their effects; besides, I should judge that it is best to listen to each other in an art which is so highly esteemed as that of playing the harpsichord.

As to the sentiment of the aspiration, it is necessary to detach the notes over which it is placed less quickly in tender and slow pieces than in those which are light and rapid.

Concerning the suspension! It is hardly used except in slow and tender pieces. The silence before the note over which it is placed must be regulated by the good taste of the person who is executing it.

AGREMENS QUI SERVENT AU JEU

C'est la valeur des notes qui doit, en general, dèterminer la durée des pincés-doubles, des ports-de-voix-doubles; et des tremblemens.

ORNAMENTS USED IN PLAYING (a)

Generally, it is the time value of the notes which ought to determine the duration of the long (double) mordent, the lower appoggiatura followed by a long mordent, and the trills. (b)

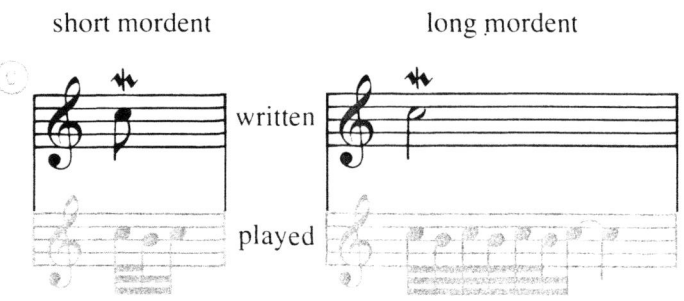

(a) The Table of Ornaments is reproduced on pages 12 and 13. A further discussion of ornaments is on pages 14-21 in the present volume.

(b) *Port-de-voix* is the term usually used to mean "appoggiatura." However, in the Table of Ornaments, Couperin shows this ornament to be an appoggiatura and mordent.

(c) In describing his ornaments Couperin is always very careful to say explicitly that they must begin on the time of their main note. Despite this, he realizes them, invariably, as though they were to be played ahead of the beat. We can only surmise that he was avoiding the complications of the mathematical problem for his readers, showing the ornaments in the clearest and easiest-to-read form and then reiterating in words that they are, nevertheless, to be played ON the beat of the main note. This, of course, is one of the most important aspects of correct performance for ornaments. The realizations made by the editor in light print reflect as nearly as possible a mathematically correct interpretation of Couperin's excellent directions.

Tout pincé doit être fixé sur la note oü il est posé: et pour me faire entendre, je me sers du terme de Point-d'arêt, qui est marqué cy-dessous par une petite ètoile; ainsi les batemens; et la note oü L'on s'arète, doivent tous être compris dans la valeur de la note èssentièle.

All mordents must begin and end on the note over which they are placed, and to make myself understood, I will use the term "stopping-point" (*point-d'arrêt*), which is marked below by a small star. So the repercussions and the note on which one stops must all be included in the time value of the main note.

exemple   pincé-double

example   long mordent

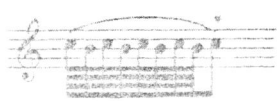

Le pincé-double, dans le Toucher de L'orgue, et du clavecin, tient lieu du martèlement dans les instrumens à Archet.

In playing the organ or the harpsichord, the long mordent takes the place of the *martèlement* on bowed instruments. (a)

Maniere pour Lier plusieurs pincés de suite par degrés-conjoints, en changeant de doigt sur la même note.

Method of slurring several consecutive mordents moving by step, by changing the finger on the same note.

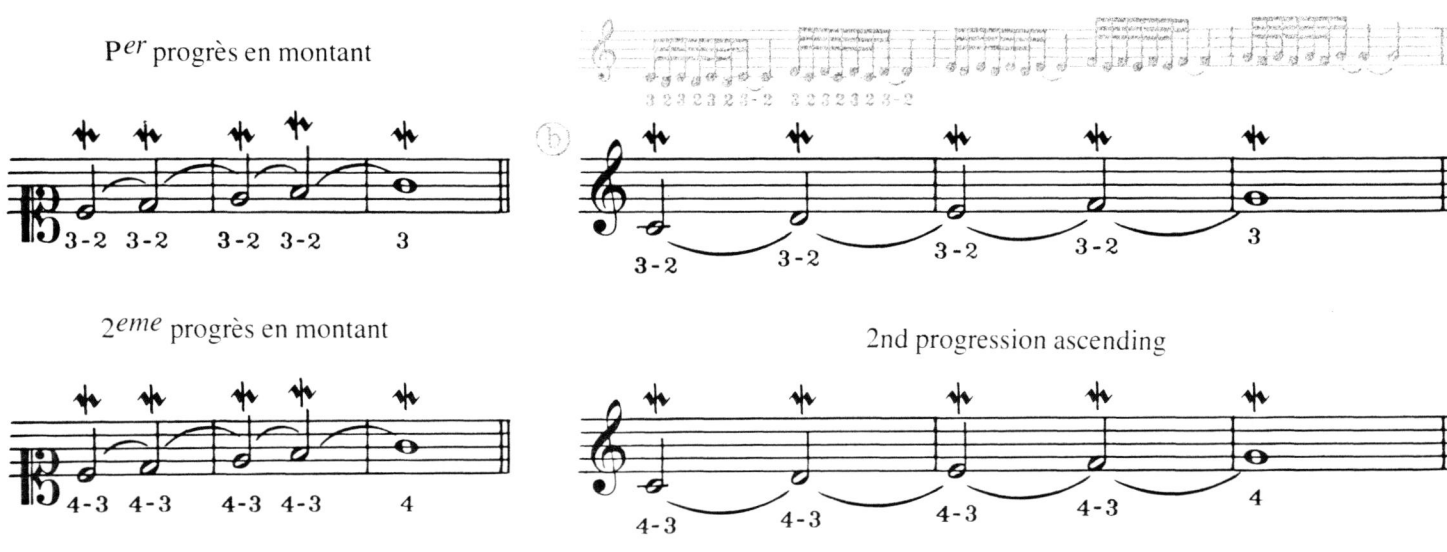

(a) The bow stroke called *martèlement*, at this period in history, was a tremolo on one note. Later, the *martèlement* became a heavily accented type of staccato.

(b) All the examples written in the moveable C-clefs have been transcribed to treble or bass clef for the modern reader's convenience.

2eme progrès en descendant

2nd progression descending

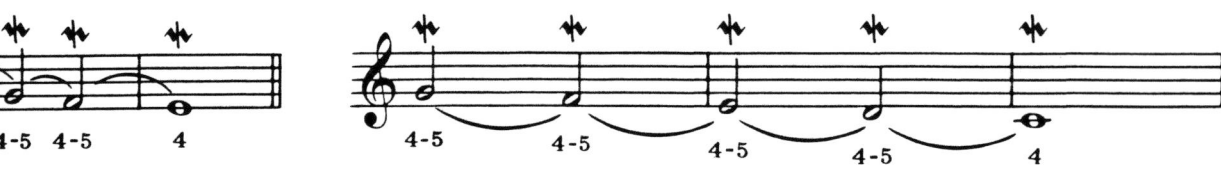

Même maniere pour les pincés-Liés de la main gauche.

Same manner for slurred mordents with the left hand.

1er progrès en descendant

1st progression descending

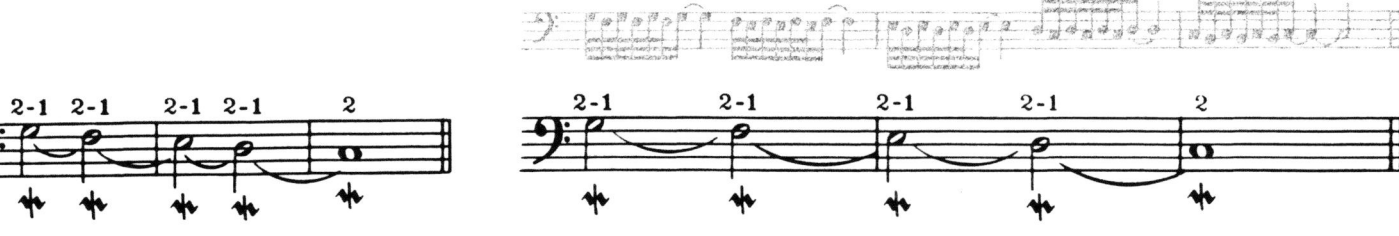

2eme progrès en descendant

2nd progression descending

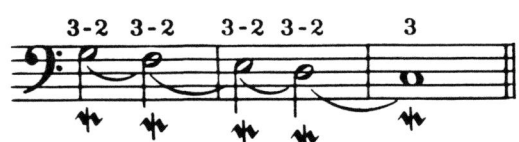

1er progrès en montant

1st progression ascending

2eme progrès en montant

2nd progression ascending

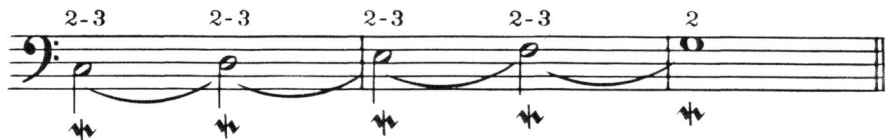

Les pincés-dièzés; et bèmolisés que j'ay introduis dans la gravure de mes pieces, ne sont pas inutiles: d'autant qu'on pouroit souvent faire les uns pour les autres, contre mon intention.

The mordents with sharps and flats which I have introduced in the printing of my pieces, are not without use; especially as one can often play one for the other, contrary to my intentions.

Le port-de-voix ètant composé de deux notes de valeur, et d'une petite note-perdüe! J'ay trouvé qu'il y à deux maniéres de le doigter: dont, Selon moi L'une est prèférable à L'autre.

The lower appoggiatura (a) consists of two notes having time value and a little 'lost note!' (b) I have found that there are two ways to finger them; however, in my opinion, one is preferable to the other.

Les notes-de-valeur des, ports-de-voix sont marquées par de petites croix dans les exemples cy-après.

The notes with time value of the appoggiaturas are marked with little crosses in the following examples.

façons modernes premier progrés		new style first progression
second progrés		second progression
façons ancienne troisiéme progrés		old style third progression
quatriéme progrès		fourth progression

Je ne passe La maniere ancienne que dans les occasions ou la main se trouve obligeé de faire deux parties differentes, allors on est trop gêné: sur tout quand les parties sont èloygnées L'une de L'autres. Où lorsque le chant vient de descendre.

I do not allow the old fingering other than places where the hand must play two different parts (at the same time). Then it is too inconvenient, especially if they are far from each other or when the melody is descending.

(a) The ornament used here, which Couperin calls *port-de-voix*, is referred to in his Table of Ornaments, reproduced on pages 12 and 13, as *port-de-voix simple*. Today we refer to it as an appoggiatura and mordent. The ornament to which we refer simply as an appoggiatura is called *port-de-voix coulée* in the Table of Ornaments. The distinction is worth noting, but does not affect the fingering principles which he is illustrating here.

(b) Couperin's delightful term *little lost note* may refer to the fact that, since all the time value in the measure is already accounted for, the little note appears to have strayed into the measure as if lost.

RAISONS DE PREFERENCE POUR LA FAÇON NOUVELLE DES PORTS-DE-VOIX

Le doigt marqué 3. dans le troisiéme progrés; et le doigt marqué 4. dans le quatriéme, étant obligés de quiter la derniere croche de valeur où il y à une petite croix, pour rebatre la petite note perduë, laissent moins de liaison qu'au premier progrés, où le doigt marqué 3. est plutot remplacé par le doigt 2., et au second progres ou le doigt 4. L'est aussi plutôt par le doigt marqué 3.

J'ai éprouvé que sans voir les mains de la personne qui joüe, je distingue si les deux batemens, en question, ont été faits d'un même doigt: ou de deux doigts différèrens. Mes élèues le sentent comme moi de là je conclus qu'il y à un vray, dont je me raporte à la pluralité de sentimens.

Il faut que la petite note perduë d'un port-de-voix, ou d'un coulé, frape avec L'harmonie! c'est à dire dans le tems qu'on devroit toucher la note de valeur qui la suit.

Il seroit tres utile de pouvoir èxercer les jeunes personnes à faire des tremblemens de tous les doigts: mais comme cela dèpend en partie de la disposition naturèle; et que quelquesunes ont plus ou moins de liberté, et de force, de certains doigts; Il faut laisser ce choix aux personnes qui les instruisent.

Les tremblemens les plus usités de la main droite se font du troisiéme doigt avec le second; et du 4.ème avec le 3.ème. Ceux de la main gauche se font du premier doigt avec le second; et du 2. avec le 3.

Quoi que les tremblemens soient marqués ègaux, dans la table des agrémens de mon premier livre, ils doivent cependant commencer plus lentement qu'ils ne finissent: mais, cette gradation doit être imperceptible.

Sur quelque note qu'un tremblement soit marqué, il faut toujours le commencer sur le ton, ou sur le demi-ton au dessus.

REASONS FOR PREFERRING THE NEW FINGERING ON LOWER APPOGGIATURAS

The 3rd finger (in the 3rd progression) and the 4th finger (in the 4th progression) were obliged to release the last quarter note having time value (where there is a little cross) in order to re-play the little lost note. This allows less legato than in the 1st progression where the 3rd finger is replaced instead by the 2nd finger and in the 2nd progression where the 4th finger is likewise replaced by the 3rd.

I have proved that without seeing the performer's hands I can distinguish if the two notes in question have been played with the same finger or two different fingers. My pupils perceive this as I do, so I conclude there is some truth in it, and I stand by the majority of opinions.

It is necessary for the little lost note of the lower appoggiatura or of an upper appoggiatura to be struck with the harmony; that is to say, during the time value of the (main) note which follows.

It will be very useful to have young persons practice trills with all fingers, but, as that depends on natural aptitude, and as some have more or less freedom of movement and strength with certain fingers, the choice must be left to their instructors.

The most frequently used trills for the right hand are played by the third finger with the second, and by the 4th finger with the 3rd. Those for the left hand are played by the first finger with the second, and by the 2nd with the 3rd.

Although the trills are written in equal note values in the table of ornaments in my first book,[a] they should, however, begin more slowly than they end; but this gradation should be imperceptible.

On whatever note a trill is written, it must always begin on the note which is a tone or semi-tone above.

---

[a] The word *premier* is not in the edition of 1716.

Les tremblemens d'une Valeur un peu considerable, renferment trois objets, qui dans L'execution ne paroissent qu'une même chose. 1. L'appuy qui se doit former sur la note au dessus de L'essentièle. 2. Les batemens. 3. Le point-d'arèst.

Trills of any considerable length have three parts, which are not the same thing in execution as in their appearance. 1. Stress (dwelling upon) which should be placed on the note above the main note. 2. Repercussions. 3. The stopping-point.

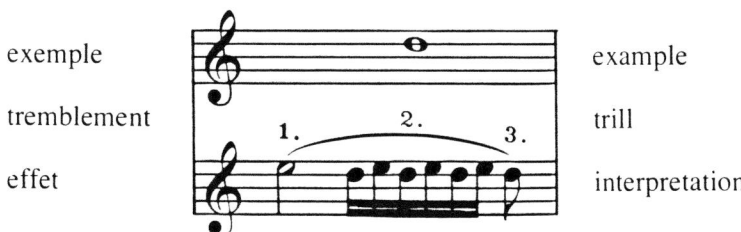

exemple — example
tremblement — trill
effet — interpretation

A L'égard des autres tremblemens ils sont arbitraires. Il y en à d'appuyés; d'autres si courts qu'ils n'ont ny appuy, ny point d'arrest. On en peut faire même d'aspirés.

Regarding other trills, they are arbitrary. There are those which have the stress (dwelling upon) on the upper note; those which are so short that they have neither stress nor stopping-point *(point d' arrêt)*. Some can even be played aspirated (followed by a short rest).

Je renvoye le lecteur aux pages 74 et 75 de mon premier livre pour le reste des agrémens qui servent au jeu; ils y sont suffisamment dètaillés; et expliqués.

I refer the reader to pages 74 and 75 of my first book for the rest of the ornaments used in playing; there they are sufficiently detailed and explained. (a)

Il marivera peutêtre dans les remarques que je ferai dans la suite, sur les endroits de mes pieces (difficiles à doigter) de reparler des agrémens, de redire Les mêmes choses; et de rèpèter les mêmes termes: mais, comme ce sera toujours à L'occasion de quelque progrès different, je préférerai L'utilité qui en résultera à la grande prècision du discours.

In the remarks I am going to make next, on the places in my pieces that are difficult to finger, one may wonder perhaps why I repeat the same things and the same terms; but as it will always be an occasion where the progression is different, I prefer the usefulness which results from great precision of language.

Avant que de passer aux petits exercices qu'il faut pratiquer pour parvenir aux pièces, on fera attention, que les tremblemens, pincés, ports-de-voix, bateries, et passages, doivent d'abord être pratiqués tres lentement; que les pièces même ne sçauroient être aprises avec trop de soin. En joüant six pièces (de differents caractères) avec règularité, on se met en état d'en joüer beaucoup d'autres; et au contraire, La quantité (aux jeunes personnes, surtout) entraine après soi un désordre dont on à beaucoup de peine à les faire revenir.

Before passing on to the little exercises which must be practiced before the pieces, take care that the trills, mordents, appoggiaturas, broken chords and passages are practiced very slowly. These pieces cannot be learned with too much care. In playing six pieces (of different characters) correctly, one will develop the ability to play many others, and, on the contrary, a larger number (of young people, above all) who practice them fast will then sound very disorderly, which will take great pains to recover from.

Il seroit bon que Les parens, ou ceux qui ont L'inspection generale sur les enfans, eussent moins d'impatience, et plus de confiance en celui qui enseigne (sures d'avoir fait un bon choix en sa personne) et que L'habile Maitre de son côté, ut moins de condescendance.

It would be well if parents or those who have the general care of children, would have less impatience and more confidence in those who teach them (being sure of having made a good choice in this person) and if the skillful Master, on his side, would have less condescension.

(a) The Table of Ornaments is on pages 74 and 75 in the first book. It is reproduced on pages 12 and 13 of the present volume. The word *premier* is omitted in the edition of 1716.

EUOLUTIONS OU PETITS EXERCICES POUR FORMER LES MAINS
EVOLUTIONS OR LITTLE EXERCISES FOR TRAINING THE HANDS

progrès de tièrces en montant — Progression of thirds ascending

en descendant / descending

progrès de quartes en montant — Progression of fourths ascending

en descendant / descending

(a) Throughout this volume, all music originally notated in the movable C-clefs has been transcribed to treble or bass for the modern performer's convenience. Breitkopf and Härtel transcribe the *Preludes* but not the *Evolutions* or the illustrative fingering passages.

(b) These two eighth notes have been changed to ♩. ♪ in the Breitkopf and Härtel edition.

(c) Each realization in light print represents one of several possibilities which would be correct according to Couperin's rules.

(d) A discussion of Couperin's inconsistency in notating afterbeats and of the custom of over-dotting appear on page 8 of this volume. Throughout the book, Brietkopf and Härtel change the number of flags on quick notes, thus radically changing the interpretation.

Manière ancienne de faire plusieurs tièrces de suitte

Old Style of playing several consecutive thirds.

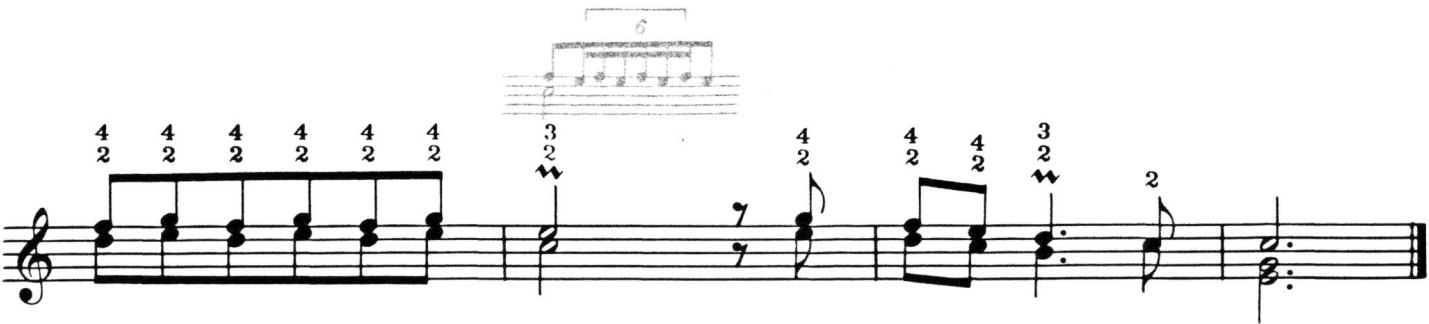

Cette Manière ancienne n'auoit nulle Liaison. Celle qui suit est la vraye.

The old style does not permit any legato. The following way is correct.

façon moderne pour couler ces mêmes tièrces.

Modern style of playing the same thirds legato.

Je suis persuadé que peu de personnes dans Paris restent entêtées des Vielles maximes; Paris étant le centre du bon: Mais comme il n'a encor paru jusqu'ici nulle mèthode qui traitte du bien-jouer, et que cellecy poura passer ailleurs, j'ai cru n'y devoir rien omettre.

I am persuaded that few people in Paris still insist upon the old maxims, Paris being the center of all that is good. But, as there has been no method until now which discusses good playing, and as this one may pass on elsewhere, I believe I ought to omit nothing.

Autre progrès de tierces coulées.

Another progression of sliding thirds.

A propos de ces tierces coulées à la moderne; Je dirai en deux mots, qu'un jour en les fesant exercer à une jeune, personne, j'essayai de lui faire batre deux tremblemens à la fois, de la même main. L'heureux naturel, les excèlentes mains; et la grande habitude qu'elle en avoit aquise, L'avoient fait ariver au point de les batre tres ègalement. J'ai perdu cette jeune personne de vuë. En verité, sy l'on pouvoit gagner cette pratique, cela donneroit un grand ornement au jeu.

About these sliding thirds played in modern style: I would say briefly, that one day, in making a young lady practice, I tried to make her play two trills at the same time with the same hand. By her natural disposition, excellent hands and much practice, she reached the point of playing trills which were very even. I have lost sight of this young lady. In truth, if one could make oneself a master of this with practice, it would be a great ornament to playing.

(a) In the edition of 1716, this portion of the sentence reads . . . *jusqu'ici ancienne methode de clavecin* . . . ' until now there has been only an old method of harpsichord playing. The remainder of the sentence is the same on both editions.'

J'en ay entendu faire, cependant, depuis, à un homme (d'ailleurs fort habile) mais, soit qu'il sy fût pris trop tard, son exemple ne m'a point encouragé à me donner la torture pour ariver à les faire comme je souhaiterois qu'ils fussent faits. Je m'en tiens, simplement, à exhorter les jeunes gens à sy prendre de bonne heure. Sy cet usage s'introduisoit, cela ne causeroit nul inconvenient pour laplûpart des pièces qui sont dèja composées, puisqu'il ne seroit question (dans de certains endroits) que d'augmenter un tremblement à la tierce de celui qui seroit marqué naturèlement.

Progrès de tremblemens enchainés, par la manière de changer de doigt sur une même note.

I have heard them played since, however, by a man (moreover with much talent), but as he had begun too late, his example does not encourage me one bit to take the necessary pains to learn to play them as I wish them to be. I simply exhort young people to take it up early enough. If this custom were introduced, it would not cause any inconvenience in the pieces which have already been composed, since it would only be a question of adding a trill on the lower note of the third (in certain passages) to the trill which is already naturally indicated.

Progression of a chain of trills by means of changing the finger on the same note.

Exemple / Example

Ces deux chifres, sur une même note, marquent le changement d'un doigt à un autre: avec la difference, que, le chifre le plus considerable ètant posé le premier, indique, qu'il faut monter en suitte; et que le moindre, au contraire, sert à descendre.

The two finger numbers on the same note indicate the change from one finger to the other, except that, when the higher number is played first, it is necessary to ascend at once, and when the lower, to the contrary, to descend.

(a) The realization in light print approximates the effect of accelerating trills. Other interpretations of this passage, consistent with Couperin's rules, are perfectly correct, as well.

progrès de tierces pour la main gauche   Progression of thirds for left hand

La même chose sur les autres tons, et demi-tons   The same thing on other tones and semi-tones

progrès de quartes   Progression of fourths

(a) A discussion of the combined trill and turn is on page 18 of the present volume. Couperin makes frequent use of this compound ornament although he does not discuss it or include it in the *Table of Ornaments*. It may also be played:

progrès de quintes — Progression of fifths

progrès de Sixiémes — Progression of sixths

bateries
broken chords

Je diray deux mots cy-apres à L'occasion des bateries

I will say a few words after this about the occurence of broken chords *(bateries)*.

progrès de septiémes — Progression of sevenths

cadence imparfaite — Imperfect cadence

autre cadence — Another cadence

autre — Another

Il est bon que ceux qui instruisent Les jeunes gens leurs insinüent insensiblement la connoissance des intervales, des modes de leurs cadences, tant parfaites, qu'imparfaites; des accords, des suppositions, cela leur forme une espece de mémoire locale qui les rend plus sures; et qui sert à les reméttre avec connoissance, Lorsqu'ils ont manqué.

A propos des bateries, ou arpègemens dont j'ay promis de parler cy devant; Et dont L'origine vient des Sonades, Mon avis seroit qu'on se bornât un peu sur la quantité qu'on en joüe sur le Clavecin. Cet instrument a ses propriètés, comme le violon a les siennes. Si le clavecin n'enfle point ses sons; si les batemens redoublés sur une même note ne lui conviennent pas extrèmement, il a d'autres avantages, qui sont, La precision, La nèteté, Le brillant; Et L'entenduë. On devroit donc prendre un milieu, qui seroit, de pratiquer quelquefois les lègèrètés des Sonades, et d'èviter les morceaux lents qui si rencontrent, dont les basses ne sont point faites pour y joindre les parties lutées, et sincopées qui conviennent au clavecin. Mais, les françois dévorent volontiers Les nouveautés, aux

It is good if those who instruct young people gradually introduce to them a knowledge of intervals, of modes and their cadences, both perfect and imperfect, of chords and chord substitutions. This will form a sort of local memory, which will make them more secure, so that when they are unsuccessful they can restore themselves by this knowledge.

Regarding broken chords *(bateries)* or arpeggios, of which I promised to speak previously, and whose origin comes from the (Italian) Sonatas, my opinion would be that the number of them played on the harpsichord should be a little restricted. This instrument has its own properties as the violin has its own. If the harpsichord cannot increase its sounds, if the repeated notes on one key are not extremely suitable, it has other advantages, which are precision, clearness, brilliance and range. One should, therefore, take a middle course, which will be to practice the rapid Sonatas sometimes, and to avoid those slow pieces which, it will be recognized, have basses which are not at all made for combining with the lute-like parts and syncopations which are suitable to the harpsichord. But

(a) There is no satisfactory literal translation for this expression. Couperin apparently refers to a reflex ability to play cadences without thinking, which is developed from practicing them many times. When the performer makes a mistake or becomes lost, he can simply cadence and then continue with a fresh start.

(b) Lute-like style included many broken chord figures and much ornamentation.

dèpens du vrai qu'ils croyent saisir mieux que les autres nations. Après tout, il faut demeurer d'accord que les pieces faites exprès pour le clavecin y conviendront toujours mieux que les autres. Cependant dans les lègéretés des Sonades, il y a des morceaux qui rèüssissent assés bien sur cet instrument. Ce sont ceux où le dessus, et la basse trauaillent toujours. Comme, par exemple: L'allemande cy-après.

the French willingly swallow whatever is novel, as they truly believe they understand better than other nations. After all, it is necessary to agree that these pieces made for the harpsichord are always more suitable for it than the others. However, it is the rapid movements of the Sonatas which are the most successful on this instrument. There are those where the bass is always moving, for example, like the Allemande which follows.

ALLEMANDE

(a) Couperin added the mordent in measure 1, the second trill in measure 6, the second mordent in measure 9, the A on the downbeat in measure 9 and the caption at the beginning of the Allemande when he revised the 1716 edition for reprinting in 1717.

Ce qui détermine les personnes médiocrement habiles à s'attacher aux Sonnades, c'est qu'il y entre peu d'agrèmens: surtout, dans les bateries: Mais, qu'en arive t'il! Ces mêmes personnes se rendent incapables pour toujours de pouvoir joüer les vrayes pièces de clavecin. Au contraire celles qui ont bien joüé des piéces d'abord, èxècutent les Sonnades parfaitement.

Avant que de passer aux remarques sur la manière de bien doigter, relatives aux endroits èquivoques de mes deux Livres de clavecin; J'ai cru qu'il ne seroit pas inutile de dire un mot sur les mouvemens françois, et la différence qu'ils ont avec ceux des Italiens.

Il y a selon moy dans notre facon décrire la musique, des deffauts qui se raportent à la manière d'écrire notre langue. C'est que nous ècrivons différemment de ce que nous èxècutons: ce qui fait que les ètrangers joüent notre musique moins bien que nous ne fesons la leur. Au contraire les Italiens ècrivent leur musique dans les vrayes valeurs qu'ils L'ont pensée. Par exemple, nous pointons plusieurs croches de suites par degré-conjoints; Et cependant nous les marquons égales; notre usage nous a asservis; Et nous continüons.

Examinons donc d'où vient cette contrariètè!

Je trouve que nous confondons la Mesure avec ce qu'on nomme Cadence, ou Mouvement. Mesure, dèfinit La quantité, et L'ègalité des tems: et Cadence, est proprement L'èsprit, et L'âme qu'il y faut joindre. Les Sonades des Italiens ne sont gueres susceptibles de cette Cadence. Mais, tous nos airs de violons, nos Pièces de Clavecin, de violes, &c. dèsignent, Et semblent vouloir exprimer quelque sentiment. Ainsi, n'ayant point imaginés de signes; ou caractères pour communiquer nos idées particulières, nous tâchons d'y remèdier en marquant au commencement de nos pièces par quelques mots, comme, Tendrement, Vivement &c, à-peu-près, ce que nous voudrions faire entendre. Je souhaite que quelqu'un se donne la peine de nous traduire, pour L'utilité des ètrangers; Et puisse leur procurer les moyens de juger de L'éxcèlence de notre Musique instrumentale.

The thing which determines people with mediocre aptitude to cling to the Sonatas is that there are few ornaments in them, especially the broken chords. Would that this would change! The same people render themselves incapable of ever playing true harpsichord pieces. On the contrary, those who have played the pieces well at first execute the Sonatas perfectly.

Before passing on to the remarks on the manner of good fingering, relative to the ambiguous passages in (a) my two books for the harpsichord, I believe it will not be useless to say a word about the animation in French music and the difference between it and that of the Italians.

In my opinion, there are defects in our method of writing music which correspond to our manner of writing our language. We write differently from the way we play, which is the reason why foreigners play our music less well than we play theirs. On the contrary, the Italians write their music in the true note values in which it is to be played. For example, we dot several eighth notes in succession moving by conjunct degrees; however, we write them in equal time values. (b) Our custom has enslaved us and we continue in it.

Let us investigate where this contradiction comes from!

I find that we confuse measure with what is called cadence. Measure is defined as the number and length of time beats and cadence is, properly, the spirit and soul which must be added to it. The Sonatas of the Italians are hardly ever susceptible to this expression. (c) But all of our airs for the violin, our pieces for the harpsichord, the viols, etc., are so designed and seem to require this sentiment. Thus, not having devised any signs or characters for communicating our particular ideas, we strive to remedy this by writing words like 'tenderly', 'quickly', etc. at the beginning of our pieces, showing pretty much how we wish them to be heard. I wish that someone would take the trouble to translate us for foreigners since, in that way, they would provide them with the means for judging the excellence of our instrumental music.

(a) The edition of 1716 reads . . . *de mon premier livre* . . . 'in my first book.'

(b) A discussion of this very important aspect of playing French music is on page 8-11 of this volume.

(c) The edition of 1716 reads . . . *ne sont point* . . . 'not at all.'

A L'ègard des pièces tendres qui se joüent sur le clavecin, Il est bon de ne les pas joüer tout à fait aussi lentement qu'on le feroit sur d'autres instrumens; à cause du peu de durée de ses sons. La cadence, et le goût pouvant s'y conserver indèpendamment du plus, ou du moins de lenteur.

Je finis ce discours par donner un conseil à ceux qui veulent rèüssir parfaitement dans les pièces! C'est d'estre deux ou trois ans avant que d'aprendre L'accompagnement. Les raisons que j'en donne sont fondées. 1°. Les basses-continuës qui ont un progrès chantant, devant être èxècutées de la main gauche avec autant de propreté que les Pièces, il est nècessaire d'en sçavoir fort bien joüer, 2°. La main droite dans L'accompagnement n'ètant occupée qu'à faire des accords, est toujours dans une extension capable de la rendre tres roide; Ainsi les pièces qu'on aura aprises d'abord, serviront à prèvenir cèt inconvènient. Enfin la vivacité avec laquelle on se porte à executer la musique à L'ouverture du Livre entraînant avec soi une façon de toucher ferme, et souvent pesante, le jeu coureris- que de s'en ressentir, à moins qu'on n'exerce les pièces alternativement avec L'accompagnement.

S'il ètoit question d'opter entre L'accompagnement, et les Pièces, pour porter l'un, ou l'autre à la perfection, je sens que l'amour-propre, me feroit prèfèrer les Pièces à L'accompagnement. Je conviens que rein n'est plus amusant pour soi-même; Et ne nous lie plus avec les autres que d'estre bon-accompagnateur: mais, quelle injustice! C'est le dernier qu'on loüe dans les concerts. L'accompagnement du clavecin dans ces oc- casions, n'est considéré que comme les fondemens d'un èdifice qui cependant soutiènent tout; Et dont on ne parle presque jamais: au lieu que quelqu'un qui excèle dans les pièces joüit seul de l'attention, et des applaudissemens de ses auditeurs.

Il faut surtout se rendre tres dèlicat en claviers; et avoir toujours un instrument bien emplumé. Je com- prens cependant qu'il y a des gens à qui cela peut estre indifferent; parcequ'ils joüent ègalement mal sur quelqu'instrument que ce soit.

Regarding tender pieces which are played on the harpsichord, it is not good to play them as slowly as if they were being played on other instruments because of the short duration of the sounds. Expression and good taste can still be preserved independently of too much slowness.

I conclude this discourse by giving some advice to those who wish to succeed in playing pieces perfectly. It is to wait two or three years before taking up accom- paniment. The reasons that I give are based on: (1) The basso-continuo which has a melodic progression to be played with the left hand, must be performed with as much neatness as the pieces, so it is necessary to know how to play them very well. (2) When playing accom- paniments, the right hand is occupied in playing chords and always in a state of tension which can make it very (a) stiff. Thus, if the pieces have been learned first, they will help to prevent this drawback. Finally, the liveli- ness with which one begins the music of the overture of the book induces a firm and heavy touch, and in play- ing, one runs the risk of feeling these effects again and again, at least unless one alternates the playing of pieces with the accompaniments.

If there were a question of choosing between bring- ing either accompaniment or pieces to prefection, I think that self-esteem would make me prefer the pieces to the accompaniment. I agree that nothing is more delightful for one's self and that nothing links one with others more than being a good accompanist, but what an injustice when he is the last to be praised at concerts! On these occasions, the harpsichord accompaniment is not considered as the foundation which supports an entire building and is hardly ever spoken of; instead, the one who excels in playing the (solo) pieces gets all the attention and the applause of the listeners!

One must always play very delicately (b) on the keyboard and always have a very well-quilled instru- ment. I understand that, nevertheless, there are those people who are quite indifferent; perhaps they play equally badly on any instrument at all.

(a) The realization of a figured bass or continuo, at this time required a considerable amount of playing triads with the right hand and the written bass line with the left.

(b) The use of more force than necessary to produce sound results in an audible thump when the jack hits the jack-rail.

ENDROITS, DE MON PREMIER LIVRE DE PIÈCES DE CLAVECIN, DIFFICILES À DOIGTER

PASSAGES IN MY FIRST BOOK OF HARPSICHORD PIECES WHICH ARE DIFFICULT TO FINGER (a)

à La Milordine, page 6, dans les 2eme et 3eme mesures de la troisiéme portée.

In *La Milordine* (I, 6), in the 4th and 5th complete measures. (b)

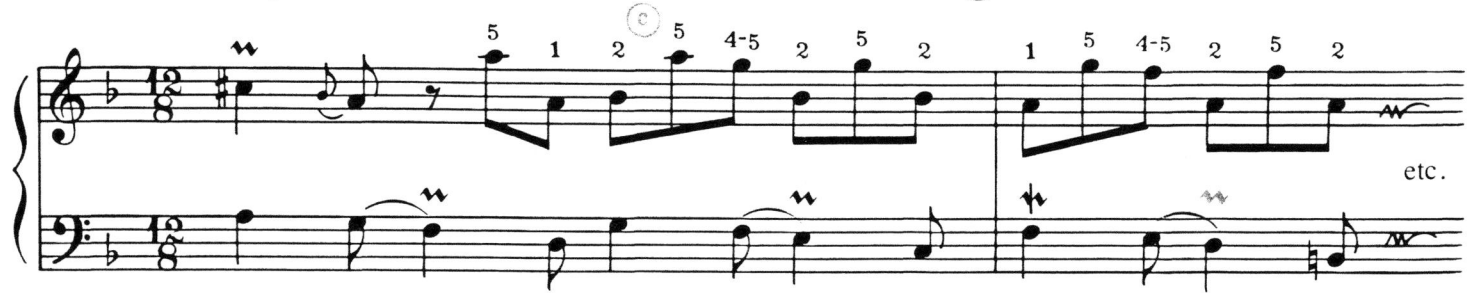

à la mème pièce, dans les pere 2eme et 3eme mesures, des 9eme et Xeme portées.

In the same piece, in the 15th through 18th measures.

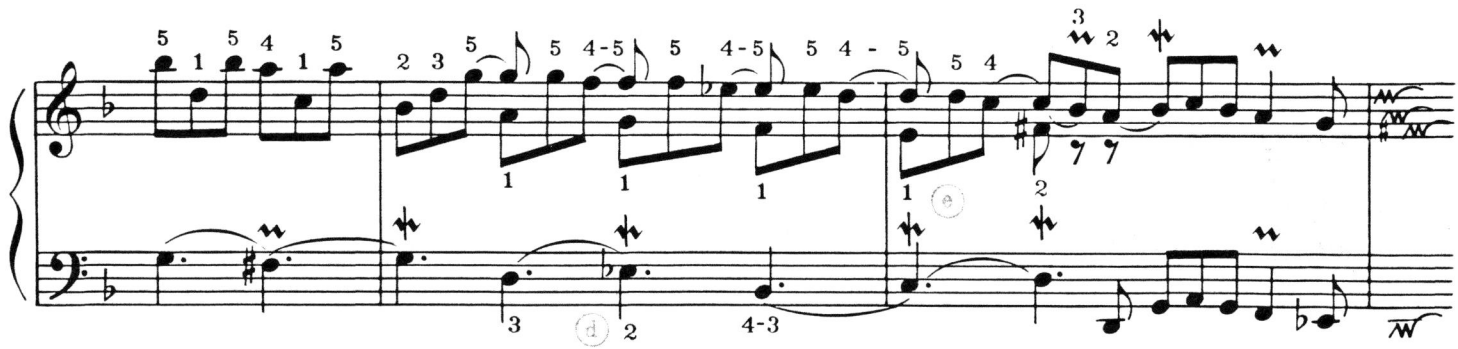

Remarqués quelle liaison Les changemens de doigts donnent au jeu! Mais, on me dira qu'il faut plus d'adrèsse que dans L'anciénne maniere. J'en conuiens.

Notice what binding (legato) the changing of fingers gives to playing! But I will be told that this requires more dexterity than the old style (of fingering). I admit it.

Dans la seconde partie des Silvains, page 9, à la 4 eme mesure de la premiere portée.

In the second part of *Les Silvains* (I, 8), the first complete measure.

(a) In the original edition of the *Pièces de Clavecin*, Couperin writes, at each of the illustrative passages contained in this book, *Voyés ma Méthode pour la maniere de doigter cet endroit* . . . 'See my method for the way to finger this passage.' There are some differences in the ornamentation in *L'Art de toucher* and in the complete pieces; however, since Couperin was illustrating fingering rather than his use of ornaments, they are not of great importance here. A discussion of Couperin's fingering and its implications of phrasing and articulation and the performance practices implied by his phrasing will be found in the Foreword to this volume, p. 21-22.

(b) The translation of the French text is: In *La Milordine*, page 6, in the 2nd and 3rd measures of the third staff. To provide the modern performer with usable information, the title of each *Pièce* is given, the *Ordre* number in Roman numbers and the chronological number within the *Ordre* in Arabic numbers.

(c) Dolmetsch omits the fingering on A, G and the last B♭ in the measure.

(d) Where ornaments are used, the fingering is for the main (written) note.

(e) Dolmetsch omits the fingering on E, F# and B♭ in this measure.

Comme la 2eme et la 4eme de ces quatre notes-coulées, sont celles qui supposent la vraÿe-harmonie contre la basse, il est necessaire qu'elles soient Touchées des mèmes doigts que si le chant ètoit simple, et sans notes d'intervales.

As the 2nd and 4th of these four notes slurred in pairs are the ones supposed to be the true harmony struck against the bass, it is necessary that they each be played with the same finger as if it were a simple melody without the passing notes.

Exemple, cy aprés

For example, the following

Ainsi, des endroits a-peu-près semblables.

Thus the passages are nearly the same.

Arpègemens dans la mème page 9, aux 7eme et 8eme portées.

Arpeggios in the same part, the first four measures of the second ending.

aux idées heureuses, page 32, dans les 3eme et 4eme portées.

In *Idees Heureuses* (II, 18), in the 3rd, 4th and 5th measures

A La grande reprise de cette mème pièce, dans les deux dernieres mesures des portées 5, et 6, et dans les premiere, et second mesures des portées, 7. et 8, qui suiuent.

Measures 7-10 in the same piece.

ⓐ The Breitkopf and Härtel edition omits the eighth note beam on these notes.
ⓑ Dolmetsch omits the substitution to the 5th finger and stops his example at the next bar line.

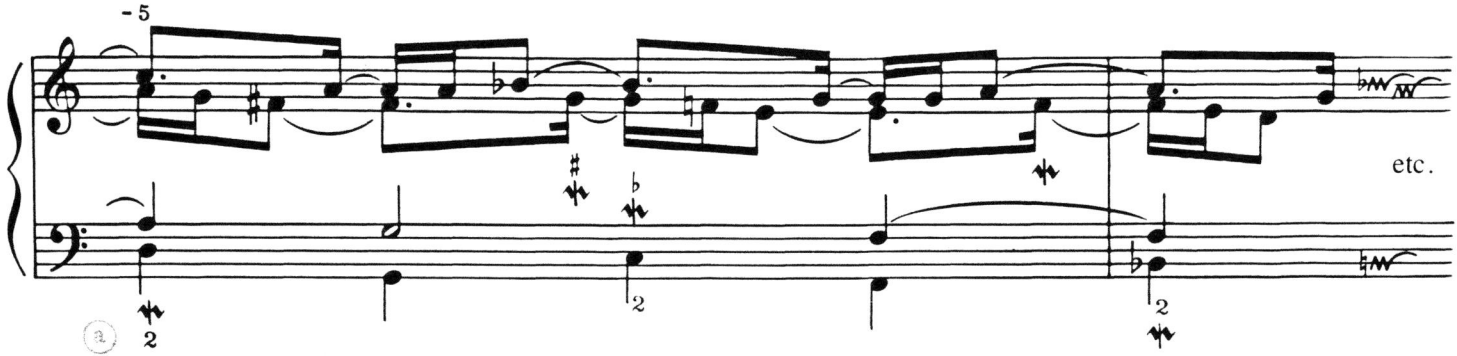

Il y a encore quelques endroits assés èpineux dans cette pièce: Mais ceux qui sont chifrés; prècédement, faciliteront pour les autres.

Dans la Courante, page 60, à la derniere mesure de la 9eme portée, et aux deux, premiere mesures de la onsiéme portée.

There are still those passages which are sufficiently tricky in this piece: but those which have just been fingered will make it easier to play them.

In the First *Courante* (V, 2), in measures 19 to 21.

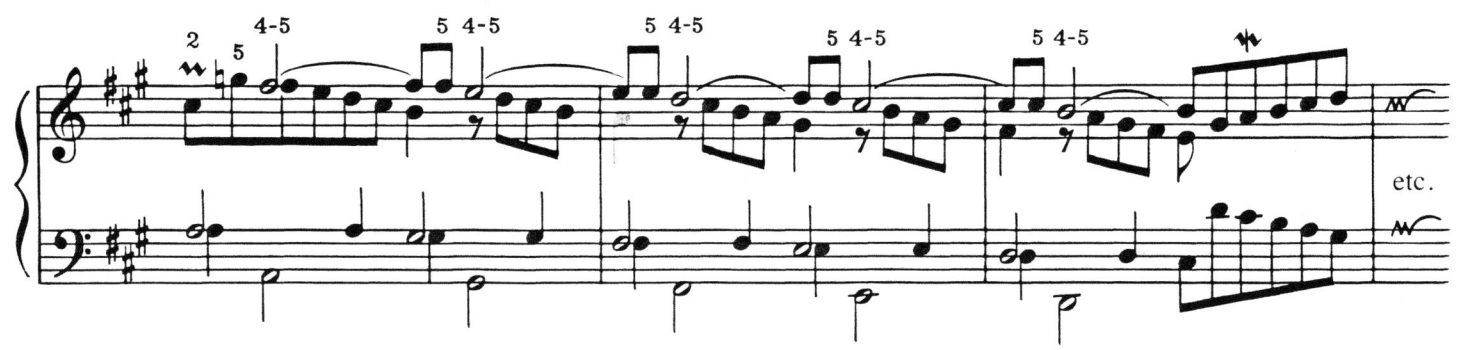

Dans la Courante page 61, Il y an un endroit semblable pour le changement du 4 au 5ème doigt

Dans La Villers, page 68, toutte la 13eme portée

In the Second *Courante* (V, 3), there is a similar passage for changing from the 4th to the 5th finger.

In *La Villers* (V, 11), measures 15 through 20 of the Second Part

(a) Dolmetsch misprints the 2 as a 3 and stops his example at the next bar line.

À L'ègard des Ondes qui est la derniére pièce de mon premier Liure, et dont L'intelligence des vrais doigts est presque necessaire dans toutte la main droite, je n'ay écrit que la plus grande partie du dessus, ou, pour mieux dire, du chant

Aux Ondes page 72, dans le premier couplet.

Regarding *Ondes*, which is the last piece in my First Book (V, 14), in which a knowledge of good fingering is necessary in nearly all the right hand, I have written the largest part of the upper portion, or, to word it better, of the melody.

In *Ondes*, in the 1st Couplet.

Dans le second couplet.

In the 2nd Couplet.

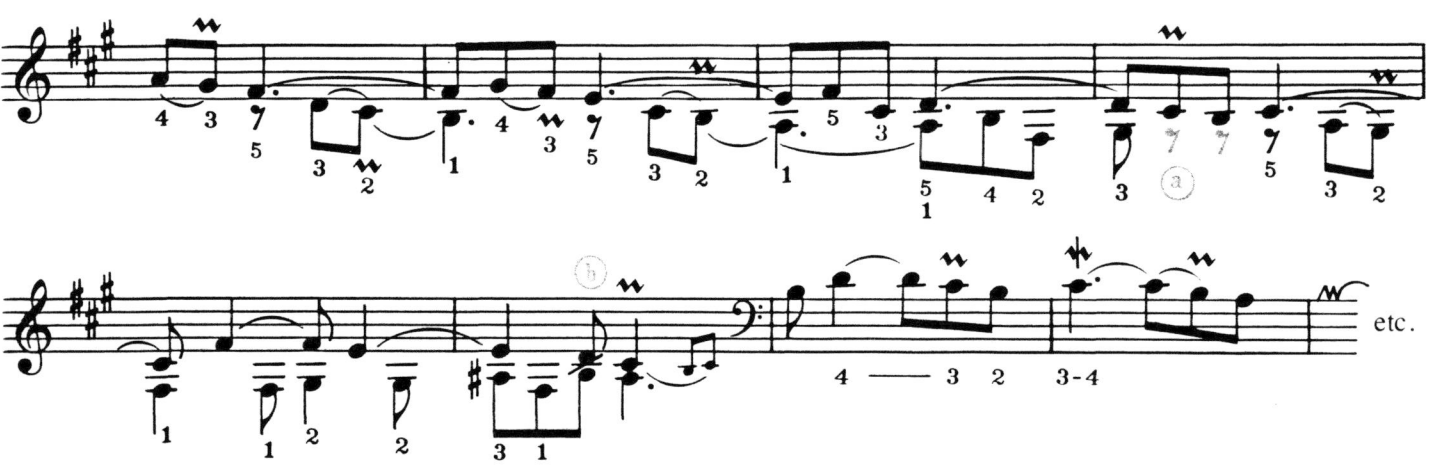

On verra dans le couplet qui suit qu'on peut faire deux notes de suite du mème doigt par degrés conjoints, quand la premiere est aspirée, ou lorsque la seconde est dans la derniere partie d'un temps

It will be seen in the following couplet that one can play consecutive notes moving by step with the same finger when the first is aspirated (half detached) or when the second is on the last part of the beat. ⓒ

3eme couplet

3rd Couplet

4eme couplet

4th Couplet

  ⓐ Neither Dolmetsch nor Breitkopf and Härtel adds the two eighth rests; Dolmetsch omits the slur and the fingering for A and G at the end of this measure.

  ⓑ Breitkopf and Härtel omit the slide between notes; Dolmetsch changes the little notes of the afterbeat to 16ths, without comment.

  ⓒ Couperin describes the aspiration on page 34. A further discussion will be found on page 18.

  ⓓ These rests are misprinted as sixteenths in the original editions.

etc.
rondeau

Fin des Renvois du premier Livre.

On trouvera ceux du second, qui vient de paroitre, en suitte des préludes cy apres.

J'ai composé les huit préludes suivans, sur les tons de mes Pièces, tant de mon premier livre; que du second qui vient d'etre mis au jour: ayant remarqué que presque toutes les ècolières de clavecin ne scavent que le petit prélude par où elles ont èté commencées. Non seulement les préludes annoncent agrèablement le ton des pièces qu'on va joüer: mais, ils seruent à dènoüer les doigts; et souvent à èprouver des claviers sur lesquels on ne s'est point encor exercé.

Les quatres premiers de ces Préludes peuvent servir à tous les âges, excepté, que pour les tres-jeunes personnes, on doit les dispenser de tenir trop-precisèment toutes les notes des accords un peu ètendus: Mais, j'en remets le choix à ceux qui leurs enseigneront.

End of references to the first book.

One will find passages for the second book, which has just been published, at the end of the Preludes which follow.

I have composed the following eight preludes in the keys of the pieces in my first book and the second which has just been published. I have noticed that nearly all harpsichord students can play nothing but the first little prelude with which they began. These preludes not only make an agreeable announcement of the key in which the pieces are going to be played; they also loosen the fingers and are often used for trying out instruments on which one has not practiced.

The first four of the Preludes can be played by all ages except very young people, who can dispense with holding down all the notes of the chords for their full time value. But I leave this choice to their teachers.

(a) Dolmetsch has added the trill without comment. There is a dot beside the note in the original editions, an apparent engraver's error.

(b) The edition of 1716 reads: . . . *tant, celles qui sont deja gravées, que celles qu'on grave actuellement ayant* . . . 'those which were previously engraved and those which I am having engraved at the present time.'

PREMIER PRELUDE   FIRST PRELUDE

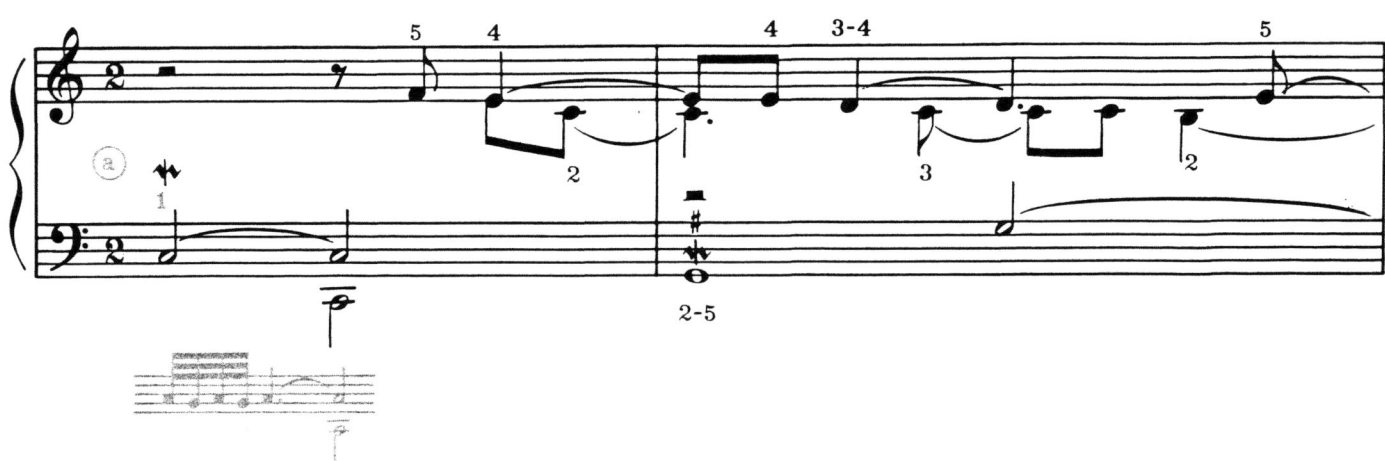

The fingering and all other markings in dark print are in the original editions. All editorial suggestions are in light print and the performer must decide for himself whether to accept or to disregard them. Realizations of ornaments represent only one of several possibilities which conform to Couperin's Table of Ornaments. A discussion of these and other related topics will be found in the Foreword.

(a) 2 is an early time signature denoting 2 rather slow beats to the measure.

(b) The dot beside Middle C is missing in the Dolmetsch edition.

(c) The tie between the first two E's is missing in the Dolmetsch edition.

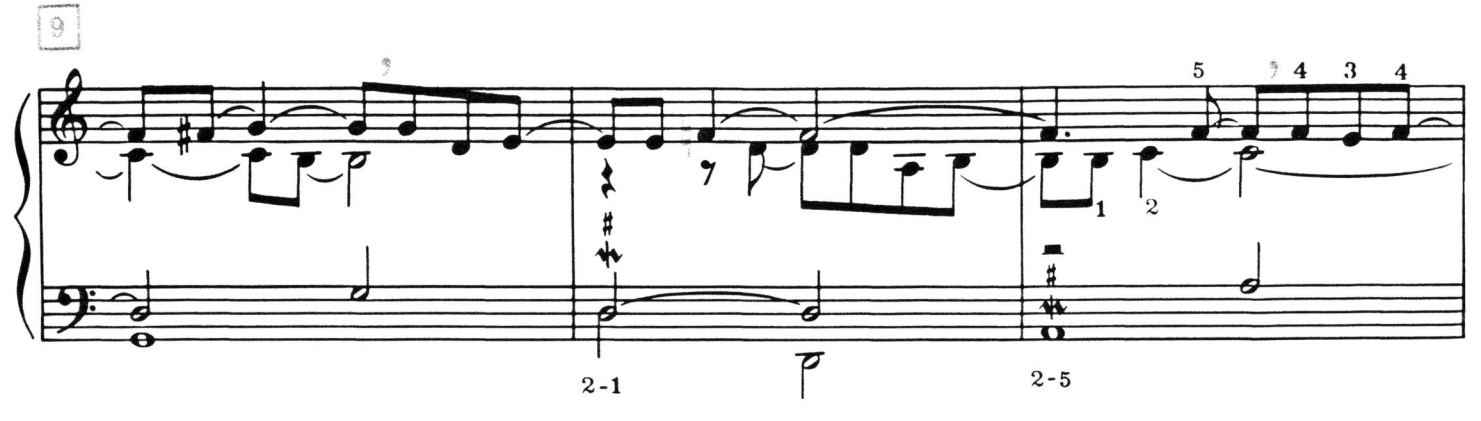
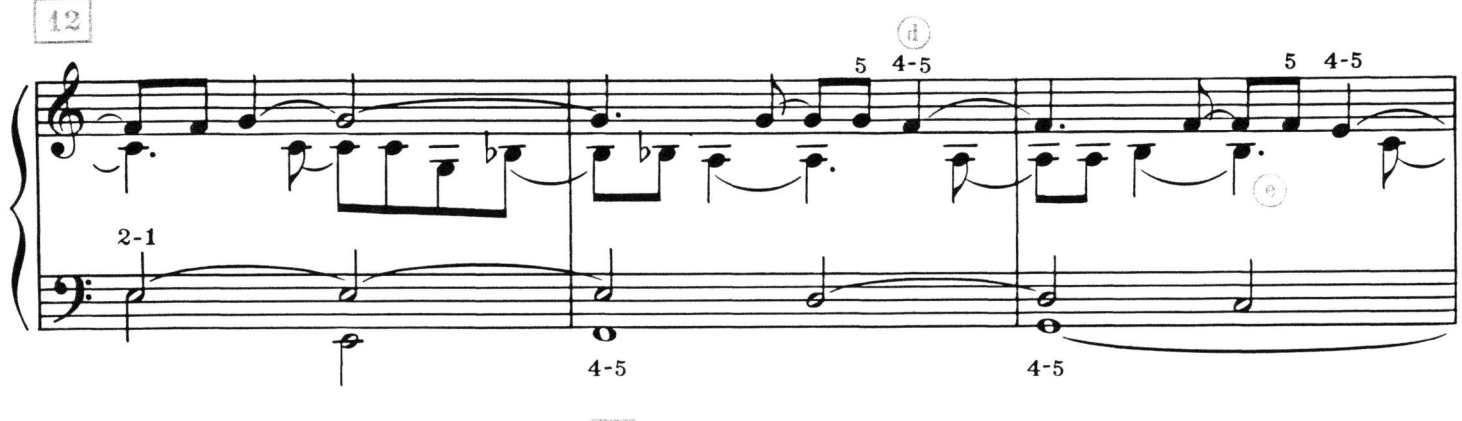

ⓓ The fingering for F is not in the Dolmetsch edition.

ⓔ The Dolmetsch edition has an eighth rest instead of the dot beside the tied B.

ⓕ In the Dolmetsch edition, middle C is an eighth note.

ⓖ The fingering for middle C is omitted from the Dolmetsch edition.

SECOND PRELUDE SECOND PRELUDE

- (a) A facsimile of the *Second Prelude* is reproduced on page 6 and a discussion follows on page 7.
- (b) The realization in light print can only approximate the custom of overdotting. See the discussion of *The Variable Dot in Baroque Music* on page 8.
- (c) This time signature is an early designation for 2 rather slow beats in a measure.
- (d) A discussion of the changes in time values on quick notes, which occurs in the Breitkopf and Härtel edition, will be found on page 8.
- (e) The slur between F and E is missing in the Dolmetsch edition.
- (f) The quarter rest is missing in the Dolmetsch edition.

- (g) The 5 in light print is misprinted as a 1 in the original edition. The remaining light print fingerings have been added by the editor.
- (h) The trill is missing in the Dolmetsch edition.
- (i) This is an eighth rest in the original editions, apparently an engraving error.
- (j) In the Breitkopf and Härtel edition, all 4 notes in the first chord are dotted. There is no dot beside the F in the original edition.
- (k) The two note slur as an indication of inequality is discussed on page 10.
- (l) The Dolmetsch edition has A instead of G for the first eighth note.

TROISIEME PRELUDE   THIRD PRELUDE

ⓐ *Mesuré* Measured (strict) time   M.M. ♩ = 84-108

ⓐ On page 70 Couperin explains his use of the word *mesuré*. See also the discussion of *Inequality* on pages 8-11.

- (b) It is suggested that both of the appoggiaturas in this measure be played as eighth notes in order to avoid consecutive fifths which are forbidden in traditional harmony. See p. 16, 19-20.

- (c) Here and in measure 17, the dot beside the eighth note should be elongated and the sixteenth note shortened as shown. A discussion of *The Variable Dot in Baroque Music* is on page 8.

- (d) The trill is misprinted as a mordent in the Breitkopf and Härtel edition.

QUATRIEME PRELUDE   FOURTH PRELUDE

ⓐ The 𝅘𝅥𝅮. 𝅘𝅥𝅯 and 𝅘𝅥𝅮. 𝅘𝅥𝅯𝅯 rhythms throughout the Prelude may be played approximately: 𝅘𝅥𝅮.. 𝅘𝅥𝅯 and 𝅘𝅥𝅮.. 𝅘𝅥𝅯𝅯. The first F for right hand may then be shortened correspondingly. The 𝅘𝅥𝅯𝅯 rhythm in measure 22 should be played approximately: 𝅘𝅥𝅯.. 𝅘𝅥𝅯 See the discussion of the *Variable Dot* on page 8.

ⓑ Although Couperin's example gives the appoggiatura half the time value of its main note, some latitude in adjusting this length to suit the context must be allowed to produce the best effect. See the discussion of Ornamentation on page 16.

ⓒ The fingering for middle C is omitted in the Dolmetsch edition.

ⓓ The 2 on G is misprinted as a 3 in the Dolmetsch edition.

ⓔ These four eighth notes are suitable for inequality. See the discussion on pages 8-11.

(g) The quick notes in this measure and in measure 22 have been changed to 32nds in the Breitkopf and Härtel edition. For a discussion, see page 8. They should be rushed in as late as possible.

Fin End

CINQUIEME PRELUDE FIFTH PRELUDE

(a) The mordent on D is missing in the Breitkopf and Härtel edition.

(b) Here and in each measure having notes with more than three beams, Breitkopf and Härtel changes them, significantly altering the effect. See the discussion on page 8.

(c) The mathematical inaccuracies involving groups of quick notes which follow dotted notes are accounted for by overdotting, a baroque custom which is explained on page 8. In performing, the dotted note is lengthened and the following quick notes played late and rushed. The approximate effect is indicated in the realizations in light print above and below the staffs.

(d) The length of appoggiaturas, usually half the value of their main note, may be adjusted to suit each particular context. Couperin describes the rhythmic freedom required by a Prelude not marked strict time, *mesuré*, on page 70. All appoggiaturas are played on the beat of the main note. A further discussion of Couperin's ornamentation will be found on pages 12-20.

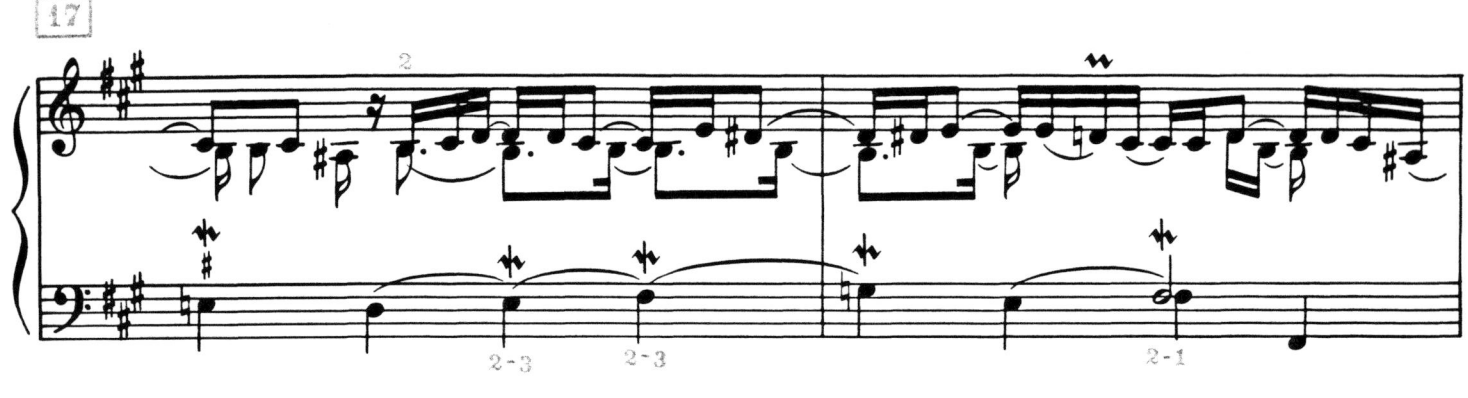
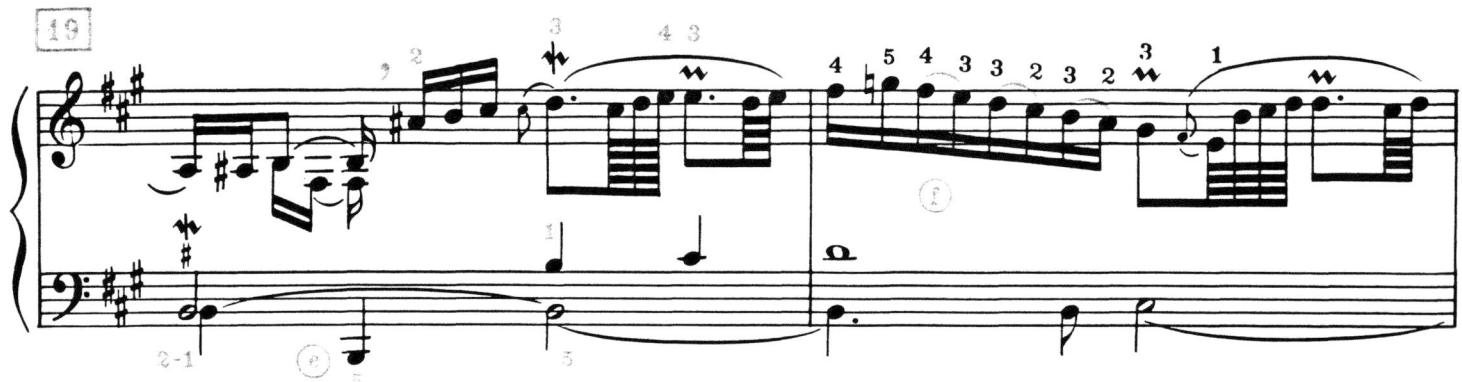

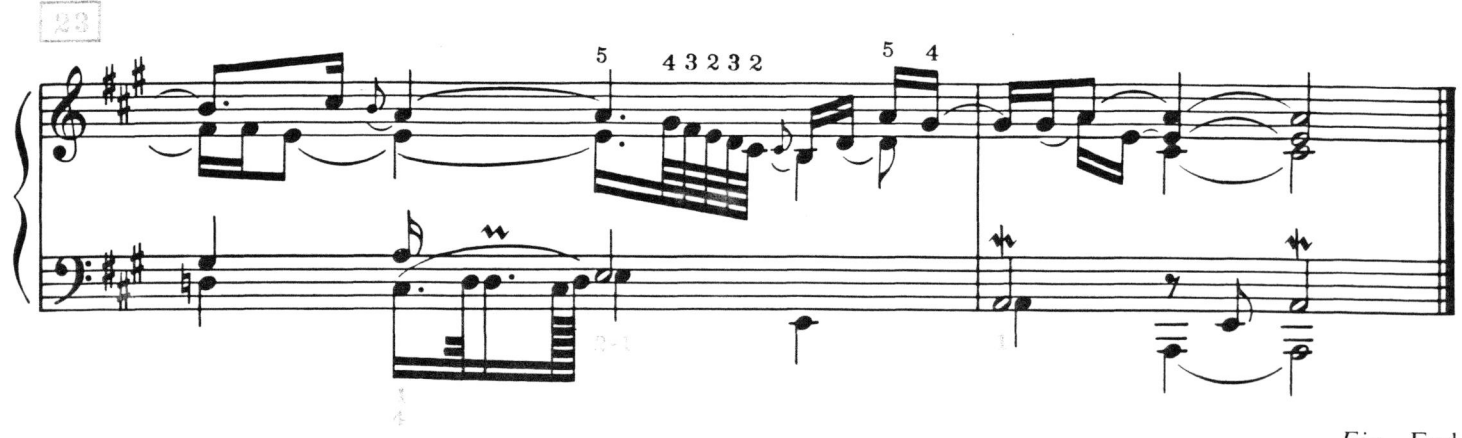

(e) The original editions have misprinted the note as low C.

(f) Couperin's fingering in this measure seems to indicate inequality. A discussion is on page 8-11.

Fin End

SIXIEME PRELUDE   SIXTH PRELUDE

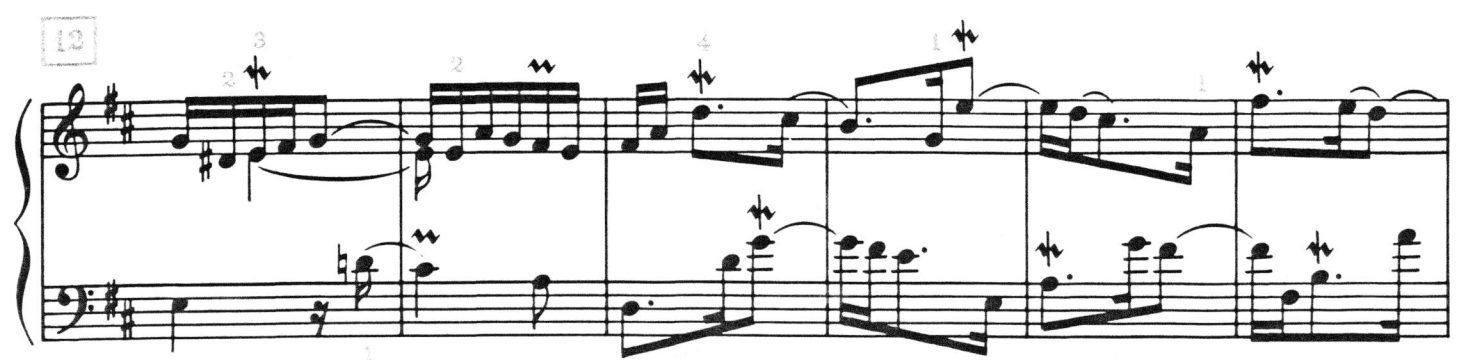

(a) Couperin describes his use of the term *mesuré* on page 70.
(b) The trill is missing in the Breitkopf and Härtel edition.
(c) Here and in measures 33, 54 and 55, the Breitkopf and Härtel edition has 32nd noted instead of 64ths.

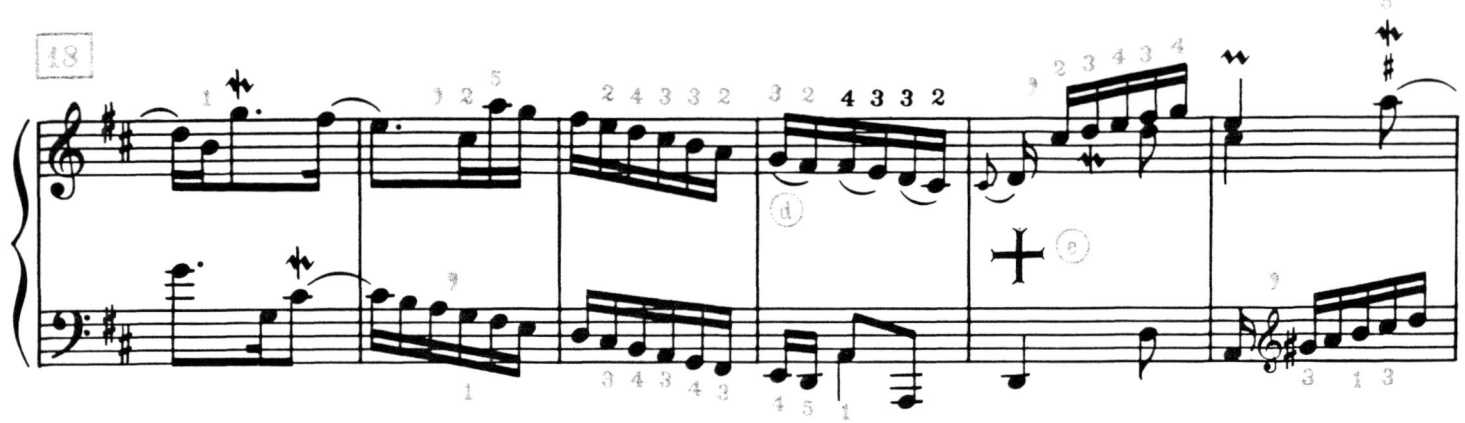

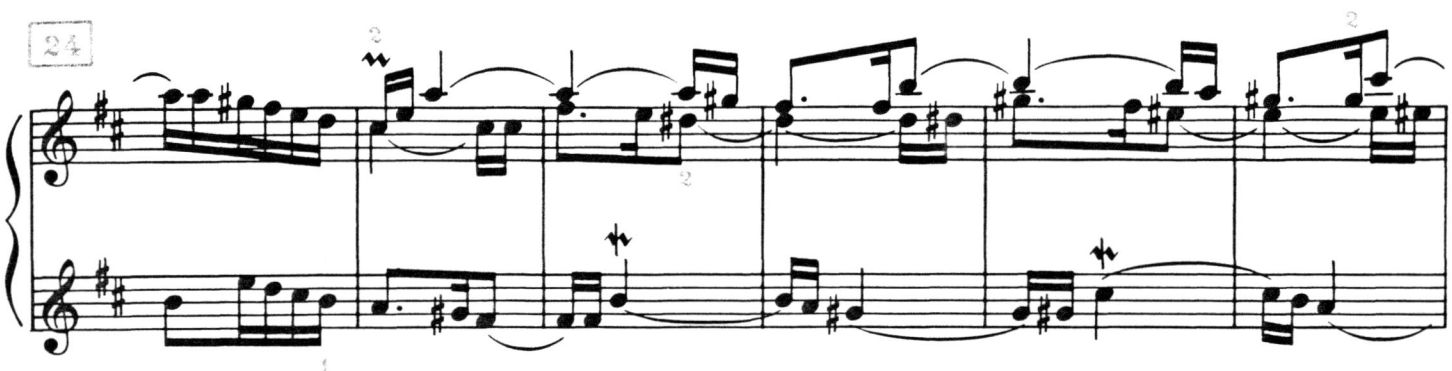

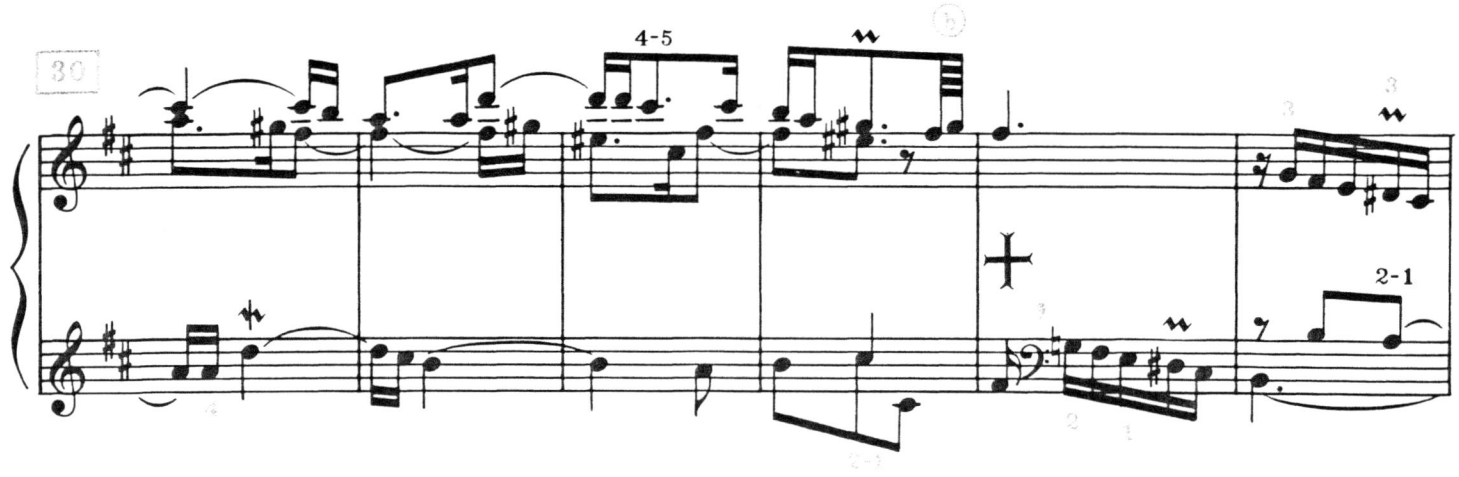

(d) The two-note slur as an indication of inequality is discussed on pages 8-11.

(e) The following directions are printed between the crosses in the original editions: *Ceux qui a'auront point de clavecin au ravalement par en hault, joueront une octave plus bas ce qui est noté d'une Croix à l'autre.* 'Those who do not have a harpsichord with a lengthened keyboard should play the passage between the crosses an octave lower than written.' Many harpsichords were built with a range of four to four and a half octaves. The process called *ravalement* was a widely used procedure in which the harpsichord case was widened to accomodate additional keys. Small harpsichords which had not been altered would not have had all the highest notes in this Prelude.

Fin End

OBSERVATIONS

Quoy que ces Préludes soient ècrits mesurés, il y a cependant un goüt d'usage qu'il faut suivre, Je m'explique. Prélude, est une composition libre, ou l'imagination se livre à tout ce qui se prèsente à elle. Mais, comme il est assés rare de trouver des genies capables de produire dans l'instant; il faut que ceux qui auront recours à ces Préludes-réglés, les joüent d'une maniere aisée sans trop s'attacher à la précision des mouvemens; à moins que je ne l'aÿe marqué exprés par le mot de, Mesuré: Ainsi, on peut hazarder de dire, que dans beaucoup de choses, la Musique (par comparaison à la Poésie) a sa prose, et ses vers.

Une des raisons pour laquelle j'ai mesuré ces Preludes, ça, èté la facilité qu'on trouvera, soit à les enseigner; ou à les apprendre.

Pour conclure sur le toucher du clavecin, en general; mon sentiment est, de ne point s'eloigner du caractre qui y convient. Les passages, les bateries, à portée de la main; les choses lutées, et sincopées, doivent être prèfèrés à celles qui sont pleines de tenües; ou de notes trop graves. Il faut conserver une liaison parfaite dans ce qu'on y èxècute; que tous les agrèmens soient bien précis; que ceux qui sont composés de batemens soient faits bien ègalement; et par une gradation imperceptible. Prendre bien garde à ne point altérer le mouvement dans les piéces-réglés; et à ne point rester sur des notes dont la valeur soit finie. Enfin, former son jeu sur le bon-goût d'aujourdhuy, qui est sans comparaison plus pur que l'ancien.

Tournés pour les autres Préludes.

OBSERVATIONS

Although these Preludes are written in measured time, there is nonetheless a tasteful custom which should be followed. I will explain. A Prelude is a composition in which the fancy can free itself from all that is written in the book. But it is all too rare to find those talents who are capable of producing this effect on the spot. It is necessary for those who will resort to the regulated preludes to play them freely without attaching too much precision to the movement; at least where I have not expressly written the word *mesuré*: thus, one may hazard to say that, in many things, music (compared to poetry) has its prose and its verse.

One of the reasons why I have measured the Preludes is that they will be found easier, whether teaching them or learning them.

To conclude about playing the harpsichord, in general, my feeling is that one should not remove himself in any respect from the character which is most suitable to it. Passages, arpeggios encompassed under the hand, pieces in lute style, syncopations, ought to be preferred to pieces which are filled with held notes of long time value or those of very low pitch. It is necessary to preserve a perfect legato in all that you play and all the ornaments ought to be very precise, and those which are made up of repercussions should be played evenly with an imperceptible speeding up; take care not to alter the rhythm in the regulated pieces and do not let go holding the notes before their time value is complete. Finally, form your playing on today's good taste, which is without comparison more pure than the old style.

Turn for the other Preludes.

SEPTIEME PRELUDE   SEVENTH PRELUDE

A facsimile of the first 12 measures of this Prelude is on page 9.

ⓐ The baroque custom of overdotting, shown in the realizations in light print above the staff, is discussed on page 8.

ⓑ In the Breitkopf and Härtel edition notes with more than three flags have been altered. See the discussion on page 8; the effect of this alteration in measure 2 is discussed on page 8.

(c) The 6 scalewise sixteenths here and the similar group in measure 9 are suitable for inequality. Although the groups of sixty-fourths in measures 22 and 23 are also scalewise progressions, the presence of the original slur on groups of more than two notes prevents inequality. A discussion of this important aspect of French baroque music is on pages 8-11.

(d) Couperin used the diagonal line between notes to indicate legato. A discussion is on page 18.

Fin End

HUITIEME PRELUDE   EIGHTH PRELUDE

(a) *Mesuré-léger*   Strict time-lightly   M M ♪ = 120-132

(a) Couperin describes his use of the term *mesuré* on page 70. See also measure 14 and footnote.
(b) Breitkopf and Härtel has a trill on C sharp. Although it is in the edition of 1716, it was removed from the edition of 1717.
(c) A discussion of Couperin's use of the diagonal line between notes to indicate legato is on page 18.

(d) The slur on the last 16th in the measure is incomplete in the Breitkopf and Härtel edition.

(e) Despite the word *mesuré*, which forbids inequality, the original two-note slurs in this measure are usually understood to indicate inequality in music of this period. Apparently Couperin wanted only the three slurred pairs in this Prelude played unequally. The performer will find the discussion of Inequality on pages 8-11 helpful in deciding whether or not to use inequality here.

(f) C has a dot beside it in the 1716 edition but it was removed from the 1717 edition. In Breitkopf and Härtel, the C in measure 18 is dotted, but the dots beside the quarter notes on the fourth beat in the next four measures (G♯; F♯; E; D♯) are missing.

FIN   END

(g)   The A is dotted in the 1716 edition but not that of 1717. Breitkopf and Härtel has the dot.

(h)   The A is a quarter note instead of an eighth in Breitkopf and Härtel.

(i)   The edition of 1716 ends here; the illustrative fingering of passages from the Second Book of *Pièces* was added to the edition of 1717. Both editions are further discussed on pages 4-5.

ENDROITS, DE MON SECOND LIVRE DE PIÉCES, EQUIVOQUES POUR LES DOIGTS.

(a) **PASSAGES FROM MY SECOND BOOK OF PIECES, WHICH ARE AMBIGUOUS IN FINGERING.**

dans les Bergeries page 8.

In *Les Bergeries* (VI, 6), the beginning of the 1st Couplet.

dans la meme piéce page 9.

In the same piece, the beginning of the 2nd Couplet.

autre endroit dans la même page

Another passage from the same piece. Measures 7-11 of the 3rd Couplet.

dans le Moucheron page 11.

In *Le Moucheron* (VI, 8), measures 3-11 after the repeat sign.

(a) The edition of 1716 concludes with the *Eighth Prelude*. A further description of the editions of 1716 and 1717, in which the passages are printed, will be found on pages 4-5 of this volume.

(b) See the explanation of finger substitution on mordents on page 35.

(c) The fingering in the original edition has two misprints. In the 5th quoted measure, the fingering for C-B♭-C reads 4-5-4 instead of 5-4-5. Couperin is known to have avoided the thumb of a raised key in passagework, as observed in his previous examples in this book, therefore, the thumb on B♭ in the last quoted measure is considered to be a misprint, and the 2nd finger the correct one. We call particular attention to this in view of the Breitkopf and Härtel edition which corrects the first misprint without comment but makes no correction on the second one. Even more curious, however, is the Dolmetsch treatment of the example. Although he carefully points out both the misprints and the corrections in an N.B., remarking that no one could mistake the thumb on B♭ as Couperin's intention if he has followed Couperin's fingering up to this point, Dolmetsch himself misprints the fingering in the second measure, where he writes 5-1-2 for the D-F♯-G group! He has changed the afterbeat to 16th notes instead of the 8th notes of the original edition, without comment.

Toute la main droite dans L'Ausoniéne, page 24.   All of the right hand of *L'Ausoneine* (VIII, 2).

Reprise

(a) The quarter rests in light print here and in measures 7, 13, 14 and 38 are half rests in the original edition.

(b) The 2 is missing in the Breitkopf and Härtel edition.

(c) The 64ths are changed to 32nds in the Breitkopf and Härtel edition.

(d) In the Breitkopf and Härtel edition, the lower stem for the first F♯ is a quarter instead of an eighth. The appearance of the original edition suggests that the eighth note flag connecting the two F♯'s may have been added after the original engraving was completed. Separately printed editions of this composition show the second F♯ as a quarter note. The text in this edition presents what appears in the original edition.

(e) The 1 on B is missing in the Breitkopf and Härtel edition.

dans la Gigue, page 30.
a la 6eme portée.

In the *Gigue* (VIII, 8), beginning at measure 11.

dans la même Piece, page 31 a la 3eme portée.

In the same Piece, beginning at measure 34.

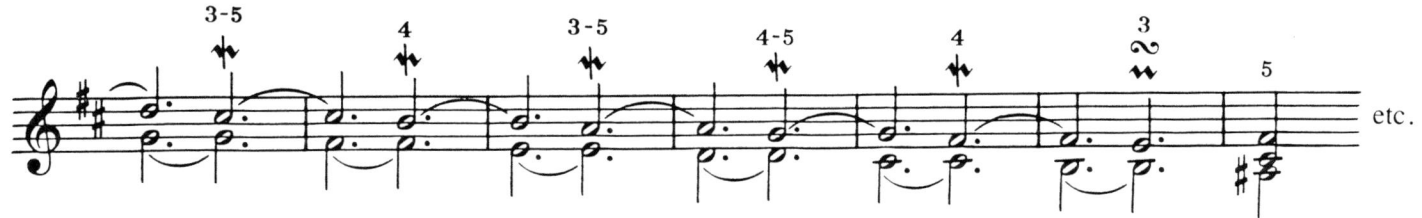

dans la Passacaille page 32 a la derniere mesure de la IIeme portée et en continüant Page 33 a la premiére portée.

In *La Passacaille* (VIII, 9), the beginning of the 3rd Couplet.

3eme Couplet

Même Page, a la 7eme portée: jusqu'a la fin du 4eme couplet.

The 4th Couplet, beginning with measure 6.

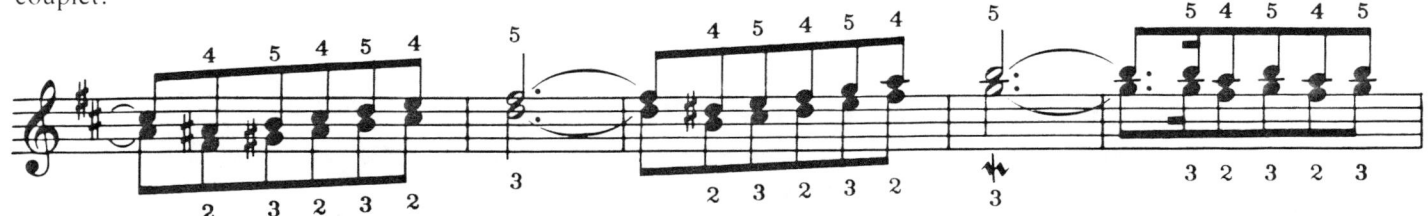

(c) Breitkopf and Härtel has a trill instead of a mordent on the F♯.

(d) The third finger is indicated in Breitkopf and Härtel but the substitution to 5 is missing.

Même Piece, page 35 au 7eme Couplet.   The same piece, beginning with the 7th Couplet.

à peu prés de même
pour la Suitte

somewhat the same
for what comes next

Dans les Charmes page 42 Toutte la main droite.   In *Les Charmes* (IX, 3), all of the right hand.

premiére partie   first part

ⓐ The Breitkopf and Härtel edition has 1 instead of 2.

ⓑ A time signature 4 is printed by mistake at the beginning of this example in the original edition.

ⓒ The fingering in the Dolmetsch book reads 1-3-5 instead of 1-2-5 on this chord.

ⓓ The 4 is missing in the Dolmetsch book.

Il faut doigter la Seconde partie avec les mêmes précautions que la premiére.

A la Seconde partie de la Triomphante page 52 dans la 3eme, et dans la 5eme portées.

It is necessary to finger the Second Part with the same precautions as the first.

In the Second part of *La Triomphante* (X, 1), beginning with measure 8.

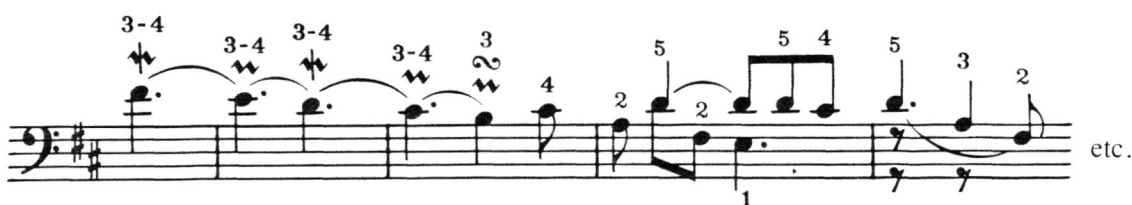

le même rangement aux endroits semblables.

The same arrangement for similar passages.

Dans la même piéce cy-devant Page 54, à la p.re et à la 2eme portées: et le même rangement dans un autre endroit qui est en suitte.

In the same piece as before, beginning with the 12th complete measure of the 1st Couplet, and the same arrangement in another passage which follows (Second Part, 3rd Couplet, beginning with the second complete measure).

(a) There are two additional finger numbers in the Breitkopf and Härtel edition: 3 is indicated for the B in measure 19 and 1 for the E in measure 20.

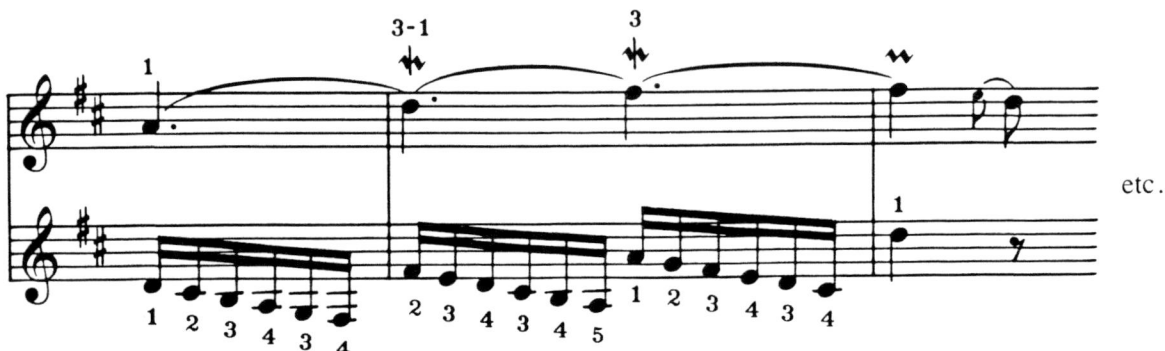

au Comencement de L'Amazône Page 61　　　　　　　At the beginning of *L'Amazone* (X, 6).

| La même chose à la 9eme portée de la même page: dans la même piéce. | The same thing, beginning at measure 17, in the same piece. |

Page 65 dans la 9eme portée. À la seconde partie des Graces-Naturéles.　　　　　　　In the Second Part of *Graces-Natureles*, (XI, 3), beginning at measure 14.

Au Commencement de la Zénobie Page 66　　　　　　　At the beginning of *La Zenobie* (XI, 4).

Le même rangement dans la reprise de cette piéce, à un endroit presque tout semblable.　　　　　　　The same arrangement in the Repeat of this piece, in a passage almost like it.

ⓐ　This ornament is a mordent instead of a trill in the Dolmetsch book.

ⓑ　The slur over pairs of notes moving stepwise is an indication of inequality. A discussion of this aspect of French baroque music will be found on pages 8-11.

au Commencement des Juméles, Page 74.　　　　　　　　At the beginning of Jumeles (XII, 1).

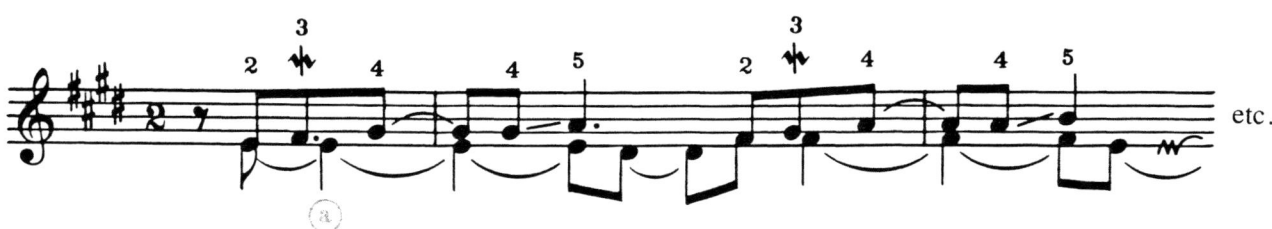

Il faut que les deux pincés, cy-dessus, soient, en quelque façon ètoufés: d,autant qu'on doit, le plus qu'il est possible, conserver la Tenüe qui est marquée dans la partie inferieure.

It is necessary that the two mordents, in the preceding example, be played in a 'stifled' manner (our accacciatura), especially since the tenuto of the lower line must be preserved to the greatest possible extent.

Dans la Reprise de L'Atalante Page 83, à la Seconde portée.

In the Repeat of *L'Atalante* (XII, 8), at measure 22.

Dans la même Page à la 4eme Mesure de la troisiéme Portée.

In the same piece at measure 30.

Dans les Xeme et derniere Portées de la même Page.

In the same piece at measure 42.

Engraved by Victor J. Mitchell

FIN　　　THE END

(a) The dot is quite clear in the original edition but the 16th flag is missing. The Breitkopf and Härtel edition has neither dot nor flag.

(b) Breitkopf and Härtel has 3 instead of 5.

(c) In the Dolmetsch book, the 4 is indicated but not the substitution to 5.

(d) In the original edition, the fingering here reads 3-1-1-3, an obvious misprint. Breitkopf and Härtel and Dolmetsch have both corrected it, but without comment.

Approbation.

J'ai lû par ordre de Monseigneur le Chancelier, L'art de toucher le Clavecin, par Monsieur Couperin: Le seul nom d'un Autheur si célèbre, doit rendre ce Livre recommandable au Public. On doit être obligé à un Maitre, qui a porté son Art au plus haut degré de perfection, de vouloir bien enseigner aux autres, par de courtes Leçons, ce qui a été en lui le fruit d'une longue Etude, et d'une application continu=elle. fait à Paris ce 20. de Mars 1716.

Danchet.

Facsimile of the Approbation from the Original Edition of 1716
Reproduced by permission of the Bibliothèque Nationale

It is probable that the Danchet who wrote the Approbation was the well known librettist who also composed an opera-ballet entitled Les Muses (1703). A translation will be found on page 5.